101 REASONS WHY YOU SHOULD NEVER LISTEN TO ANYONE

G. R. HOWARD

ROCKWELDER PRESS

DALLAS

ISBN: 978-0-9972373-4-4

Cover design by Mark Hesselgrave

Printed in the United States of America

First Edition: January 2017

www.wrong101.com

Foreword

THIS IS A simple book I wrote with the idea that anyone could pick it up from a coffee table in a doctor's or dentist's office, off a bookshelf, off the Internet, or anywhere for that matter, and within a couple of pages, be inspired.

There are a lot of motivational books out there, with many of them dedicated to providing the reader with an array of skills to be successful. This book does no such thing, other than to present example after example of what I consider the two most important skills: perseverance and the ability to filter out noise.

You see, every significant scientific or technological advance became manifest amidst an audience of naysayers. Every person who ever amounted to anything, every dedicated dreamer, every doer, every person who was set on accomplishing something of importance did so in the presence of those who said he or she couldn't do it. Every one of them.

Whether it were friends, family, colleagues, the "experts," or even at times the persons themselves, there was always somebody, and more often than not, a chorus of somebodies, who said "it" couldn't be done.

This book is dedicated not to the ones who have defied the odds, but to the ones who will. Criticism is inevitable; persistence is supreme. Dream on. Keep paddling.

G. R. Howard

P.S. – If you actually think there are 101 reasons in this book, you would be wrong. There are, in fact, 102.

Acknowledgments

Whatever my shortcomings, I somehow have been blessed with the best friends a human being can possibly imagine. Every step I take in this life is with the knowledge that good people will be there for me no matter what happens. And they proceed knowing the same. It is because of them that I am able to bring this book to you.

Table of Contents

WRONG!

"Come to me, and I will give thy flesh unto the fowls of the air, and to the beasts of the field."

— *GOLIATH, TO DAVID*

A PARTICULARLY BAD prediction, as the person who said it died immediately thereafter. The mighty Philistine warrior Goliath was felled by a single, accurate stone from the sling of the shepherd boy, David, who wasn't even a member of the Israelite army, but was merely bringing food to his brothers.

Goliath's career was over, but David's was just beginning. He became a successful general, and then was crowned the second king of the united Kingdom of Israel. He is a revered figure in the religions of Judaism, Christianity, and Islam.

In his spare time, he played the harp and wrote psalms.

“Alva is addled and it would not be worthwhile keeping him in school any longer.”

— *THOMAS ALVA EDISON’S TEACHER AT PORT HERON ELEMENTARY SCHOOL, TO SCHOOL INSPECTOR*

AFTER ALVA OVERHEARD this conversation, he reported it to his mother, who promptly took him out of school and gave her son a healthy dose of home education.

Addled Alva Edison later decided to go by his first name, and Thomas became one of the most prolific inventors in history, holding 1,093 U.S. patents, as well as many patents in the United Kingdom, France and Germany. Aside from the "simple" invention of the first practical light bulb, the "Wizard of Menlo Park" brought us devices such as the phonograph, the motion picture camera, the alkaline battery, and many, many others.

"Who'd be stupid enough to buy a thing like that when he can buy a horse?"

— WILLIAM FORD, TO HIS SON, HENRY

ALTHOUGH HE DID not like working on his father's farm, Henry Ford did learn there was great value in working hard. He preferred to work with mechanical objects, particularly watches.

As an adult, Ford was employed by the Edison Illuminating Company, and spent his spare time designing an automobile with an internal combustion engine. In 1899, the Edison Company forced Ford to choose between automobiles and his job. He did, and ten years later, rolled out the "Model T."

In 2010, the number of automobiles in the world topped the 1 billion mark.

"You haven't it in you, Georgie; take my word for it, I can tell!"

— MAXIE ROSENZWEIG (AKA MAX ROSEN), CHILD PRODIGY & WORLD-RENOWNED VIOLIN PLAYER, ON GEORGE GERSHWIN'S FUTURE AS A MUSICIAN

INITIALLY, GEORGE GERSHWIN had no interest in music. Then at the age of ten, he overheard Maxie playing violin at a music recital at school. Describing the event later as a "flashing revelation of beauty," George turned his attention to the family piano.

When he was fifteen, Gershwin quit school and took his first job as a song plugger for Jerome H. Remick and Company, a song publishing firm on New York City's Tin Pan Alley. For this, he earned the princely sum of $15 a week (equivalent to $350 a week in 2015).

With his brother Ira providing lyrics, Gershwin composed many tunes which have become popular music standards including "I've Got Rhythm," "I've Got A Crush On You," and "Summertime."

In 1924, Gershwin composed his first major classical work, *Rhapsody in Blue*, for orchestra and piano. *Porgy and Bess* premiered in a Broadway theater in 1935 and is now widely regarded as the most important American opera of the twentieth century.

The breadth of his accomplishments was immense: musicals, film scores, classical pieces, and more than 800 songs. Gershwin did all this before his untimely death at the age of thirty-eight.

"There's no way you can make it in Chicago up against Donahue. It's his home base. You're walking into a land mine and you can't even see it. You're committing career suicide. You're going to fail."

— PAUL YATES, GENERAL MANAGER OF WJZ-TV, BALTIMORE

OPRAH WINFREY BEGAN her career in Baltimore where she co-hosted a successful morning talk show for eight years. Chicago station WLS offered her an audition for its *AM Chicago* show over Labor Day Weekend in 1983.

Winfrey aced the audition. In a conversation that seems incredible now, she laid bare her concerns about being African-American and overweight with the station's general manager, Dennis Swanson. Swanson told her not to worry. He sensed she was genuine and predicted that audiences would feel the same. He also told her not to worry about beating Donahue, as the station had no illusions about that happening.

In Baltimore, Winfrey had regularly beat Donahue. In just one month in Chicago, she did it again. *AM Chicago* was changed to *The Oprah Winfrey Show* and went national shortly thereafter. As of 2013, it is the highest-rated talk show ever.

Mr. Swanson has had a distinguished career in broadcasting, and he became Chief Operating Officer at CBS in 2002.

Winfrey has gone on to become a businesswoman extraordinaire, a media mogul, and a philanthropist. In her spare time, she was nominated for Best Supporting Actress in *The Color Purple*.

“The Yankees will have to build a park in Queens or some other out-of-the-way place. Let them go away and wither on the vine.”

— JOHN MCGRAW, MANAGER OF THE NEW YORK GIANTS

MCGRAW, HAVING ALREADY gained respect as a tenacious ballplayer and archetypal baseball manager, was perturbed by the situation at the Polo Grounds, the home stadium for his New York Giants. The Giants, the premier baseball team in the National League, had rented use of their ball park to the New York Yankees of the American League from 1920–1922. The Yankees, having purchased a young slugger from Boston named Babe Ruth, had the audacity to outdraw the Giants in attendance over those years by a healthy clip. Even though the Giants had defeated the Yankees in the previous two World Series, McGraw found the situation intolerable and promptly told the Yankees they were no longer welcome.

In 1923, the Yankees opened Yankee Stadium less than a mile away across the Harlem River. They won their first World Series that year. Their opponent: the New York Giants.

In the years since McGraw's decision, the Giants have managed to win five championships. Three of those titles were won in California. The New York Giants, despite having baseball's most exciting player in Willie Mays, moved to San Francisco in 1958 due to low attendance.

The Yankees continue to whither right across the river from where they were evicted. In the meantime, they have won twenty-seven championships and built a new Yankee Stadium.

"You're a very clever boy, Einstein. An extremely clever boy. But you have one great fault: you'll never let yourself be told anything."

— HEINRICH FRIEDRICH WEBER, ONE OF TWO PHYSICS INSTRUCTORS AT THE EIDGENÖSSISCHE POLYTECHNISCE HOCHSCHULE

"He always does something different from what I have ordered."

— JEAN PERNET, THE OTHER PHYSICS INSTRUCTOR AT THE EIDGENÖSSISCHE POLYTECHNISCE HOCHSCHULE

CONTRARY TO MYTH, Einstein never failed math in school — he failed physics! Though bright, Einstein demonstrated an independent streak, and he showed little interest in studying things he considered below his level. Accordingly, Professor Pernet gave Einstein the lowest possible grade in his Physical Experiments for Beginners class. At Pernet's request, Einstein was given a reprimand "due to lack of diligence in physics practicum."

Six years later, while still a clerk in a patent office and with limited access to reference materials, Einstein published four articles in the *Annalen der Physik* that revolutionized science. The first dealt with the photoelectric effect, wherein Einstein proposed that energy was released in specific amounts called quanta, thereby laying the groundwork for what came to be known as quantum mechanics. He later won the Nobel Prize for this work.

With the publication of the next three articles, Einstein presented his Special Theory of Relativity and formulated mass-energy equivalency with the most famous equation in the world: $E=mc^2$. Because of these four revolutionary articles, scientists refer to the year 1905 as *Annus Mirabilis* (the Miracle Year). In 1915, Einstein presented his General Theory of Relativity, putting forth the radical notions of gravitational and inertial equivalence, time dilation, bending light rays, and space curvature.

As radical as Einstein's ideas were, they have all been verified by later scientific experiments.

"...personally brave and energetic to a fault, he yet is wanting in moral firmness when pressed by heavy responsibility and is likely to be timid and irresolute in action."

— UNION GENERAL GEORGE MCCLELLAN, ON CONFEDERATE GENERAL ROBERT E. LEE, 1862

SHORTLY AFTER TAKING over the Army of Northern Virginia, General Lee attacked McClellan's troops, which were stationed around Richmond, and it was McClellan who proved timid and irresolute. While McClellan was busy petitioning Washington for unnecessary additional troops, Lee chased McClellan off the peninsula, then boldly split his army and crushed another Union army at the Second Battle of Bull Run. He later used the same daring tactic at the Battle of Chancellorsville.

In short order, Lee proved himself to be one of the greatest commanders in the history of warfare. Lee gave a series of Union commanders fits until he was opposed by the drunkard Ulysses S. Grant.

"Our noble army of the Mississippi is being wasted by the foolish, drunken, stupid Grant. He cannot organize or control or fight an army. I have no personal feeling about it; but I know he is an ass. There is not among the whole list of retired major-generals a man who is not Grant's superior."

— MURAT HALSTEAD, EDITOR OF THE CINCINNATI GAZETTE, TO TREASURY SECRETARY SALMON P. CHASE

ULYSSES S. GRANT GRADUATED without distinction from West Point in 1843, and served in the army until 1854. A venture into civilian life was not at all successful, as he failed at his attempts at farming and real estate. He ultimately had to take a job as a clerk at his father's tannery in order to support himself and his family.

Yet when the Civil War broke out in 1861, Grant quickly proved himself to be the Union's ablest general. He took Forts Henry and Donelson in 1862 in the first major Union victories of the Civil War. The following year he led a brilliant campaign to take the strategic city of Vicksburg, which gave the Union control of the Mississippi River and split the Confederacy in two.

After these successes, he was given command of the Army of the Potomac, which had repeatedly suffered defeats at the hands of Robert E. Lee's Army of Northern Virginia. Within a year of Grant taking command, Lee had surrendered and the war was over.

President Lincoln, when informed that General Grant preferred to guzzle whiskey while leading his troops, famously asked for the name of the brand so he could send it to his other generals.

U.S. Grant later went on to become the eighteenth president of the United States.

"There's no money to be made there. Why is that an interesting business?"

— BILL GATES, MICROSOFT CEO,
REGARDING THE INTERNET,
APRIL 1994

BILL GATES AND Microsoft had achieved dominance in the computer market by licensing the operating systems DOS and Windows. By bundling an office suite with the product, Microsoft had a virtual monopoly on personal computing software. In the meantime, what had started out in 1969 as ARPAnet, a small network for four mainframe computers to communicate, was now coming of age as the Internet. Soon businesses were taking advantage of it and commercial sites began to appear.

Six months after Gates' observation, Netscape Navigator, a web browsing software, hit the market and soon commanded 90 percent of all web traffic. In August 1995, Netscape experienced one of the most impressive initial public offerings ever, when its stock value more than doubled in a single day.

Gates could see that the Internet was dramatically altering not just the computing business, but every business, and that the Internet as a platform could seriously threaten Microsoft's dominance. Gates issued a memo to the company titled "The Internet Tidal Wave" and Microsoft made the Internet priority number one. Investing millions of dollars and again bundling the software with the operating system, Microsoft presented its own browser, Internet Explorer. By 2003, Internet Explorer had 95 percent of the browser market. When Microsoft decided in 2015 to replace Internet Explorer with its new Edge browser, Internet commerce amounted to better than $3 trillion a year.

“Entre nous, a certain great man is damnable deficient.”

— *GENERAL CHARLES LEE, ON GEORGE WASHINGTON, DECEMBER 12, 1776*

GENERAL CHARLES LEE, second in command to Washington, was often quite critical of his superior, and he was not alone. Another Revolutionary War leader, James Reed, made no secret of his disapproval of General Washington's leadership. Dissent was quite common in the troops of the Continental Army.

General Lee's comments were ill-timed, as British soldiers arrested him in a tavern shortly thereafter. Less than two weeks later, the deficient Washington scored a brilliant victory at Trenton, providing a pivotal impetus to the quest for American independence.

"The man who has made the mile record is W.G. George...His time was 4 minutes 12.75 seconds and the probability is that record will never be beaten."

— HARRY ANDREWS, 1903

IN A RACE at Oxford University on May 6, 1954, Roger Bannister crossed the finish line in 3:59.4, laying to rest the myth that the four-minute mile was impossible.

Despite his landmark achievement, it is no longer extraordinary. The four-minute mile has been broken more than 5,000 times by more than a 1,000 men. In 1999, Hicham el-Guerrouj of Morocco would have left Bannister more than 100 meters behind when he set the current world record of 3:43.13. Mr. George would have been another 80 meters to the rear.

“Anyone with a bandsaw could have put it together.”

— TED MCCARTY, PRESIDENT OF GIBSON GUITARS

IN THE LATE 1940s, when guitarists of the day were searching for more volume, Gibson and other established guitar makers responded by adding an electronic "pickup" into various acoustic models. While these did offer more volume, they were prone to feedback. Meanwhile, Leo Fender and his fledgling Fender Guitar Company had developed a solid-body design that, unlike other individually-crafted guitars, was meant to be mass-produced.

The Fender Esquire made its debut at the 1950 NAMM show. With its color an uninspiring washed-out blonde and its neck a solid piece of maple bolted onto the body, it was derisively called by other guitar makers a "canoe paddle" and a "snow shovel."

But it was the ultimate utilitarian guitar. If you broke the neck, you just screwed on another. It had a rich, trebly, bell-like tone that sounded unlike other guitars and could cut through any mix. A second pickup was added, and after a brief life as the Broadcaster, it finally went to market as the Telecaster. Its success prompted Gibson to introduce the Les Paul model in 1952.

Leo Fender followed the Telecaster with the Precision Bass, the first bass that could be played like a guitar, the futuristic Stratocaster guitar, and a line of amplifiers that set the industry standard.

For the record, Leo Fender could not play guitar.

"We don't have a chance against these guys."

— GARY SMITH, TRAINER FOR THE 1980 U.S. OLYMPIC HOCKEY TEAM

AND MR. SNYDER was right. For on that day, the U.S. Olympic hockey team got routed 10–3 in an exhibition game by the team from the Soviet Union. But what would you expect? The Soviets were 27–1–1 in the previous four Olympics. A year earlier, the Soviet national team had routed the National Hockey League All-Stars, 6–0.

The U.S. squad was made up of collegiate players, but coach Herb Brooks had done an outstanding job of getting them physically and mentally ready. But how would they react to the throttling just a week before the Olympics?

In their first game against favored Sweden, the U.S. earned a dramatic 2–2 tie by scoring with thirty seconds left in the game. Then came a 7–3 upset over Czechoslovakia, followed by three more wins to advance to the medal round where they were to meet the Soviets, who had been annihilating opponents.

The U.S. was outshot 39–16, but somehow tied the game early in the third period. Team captain Mike Eruzione then fired a slapshot to put the American team up 4–3 with ten minutes to play. The U.S. held on for the win and went on to capture the gold medal by beating Finland.

The Soviets would not lose another international game for five years. The American victory was voted the greatest sports moment of the twentieth century by Sports Illustrated.

"The countries of Eastern Arabia thus traversed do not present any decided promise for drilling on oil."

— *ARNOLD HEIM, GEOLOGIST, 1924*

OIL WAS FIRST discovered in the Middle East in northwestern Persia in 1908, but early projections for the Arabian Peninsula were not encouraging.

Despite opinions to the contrary, a passionate and persuasive New Zealander, Major Frank Holmes, was convinced that oil would be found in the region. In 1925, after Holmes was successful drilling for fresh water, the Sheikh of Bahrain awarded him a concession, enabling him to search for oil there. Holmes then went to the United States to seek an oil company that would be interested in the concession. Initially, Gulf Oil was, but due to a contractual conflict, the company had to transfer its interest to Standard Oil of California (SOCAL), now known as Chevron.

In 1932, SOCAL struck oil in Bahrain, and then won a bidding competition for a concession in Saudi Arabia.

On March 3, 1938, oil was struck. In 1948 at Ghawar, the largest oil field ever was discovered. It still pumps 5 million barrels a day.

"You all better make it light on yourselves and let me have those seats."

— *JAMES FRED BLAKE, MONTGOMERY BUS DRIVER*

THREE OF THE passengers obliged, but the incident is famous for the one who didn't.

In 1955, the seating in buses in Montgomery (and all of Alabama) was segregated: white people sat in the front and black people sat in the back. However, if a surplus of whites came onboard, blacks were expected to give up their seats to the whites.

Rosa Parks refused to give up her seat, and was arrested. Parks was secretary of the local chapter of the NAACP. The president of the Montgomery chapter, Edgar Nixon, bailed her out the following day, and then began calling local ministers to support a boycott of the buses by black citizens of Montgomery. One of the ministers, Martin Luther King Jr., a recent transplant from Atlanta, quickly rose to fame and later received a Nobel Peace Prize for his practice of non-violent protest.

Showing remarkable solidarity and perseverance, the African-American community avoided their primary form of transportation for 381 days. In November 1956, the Supreme Court of the United States upheld a lower court ruling in the case *Browder v. Gayle* that Montgomery's law on bus seating was unconstitutional. The following month, after rejecting appeals, the Court ordered the buses desegregated.

The boycott had worked. The Civil Rights Movement had begun.

“Steve Jobs is the problem. Tell Steve that he is destroying Apple!”

— RICH PAGE, APPLE LISA HARDWARE ENGINEER

STEVE JOBS WAS co-founder of Apple. In 1982, Jobs had been working on the Lisa, an innovative high-end computer that Apple had high hopes for. Due to infighting, he was removed from the Lisa team and assigned to take over another computer line: the Macintosh. When Jobs started using valuable company resources to finish the "Mac," Page made his famous comment.

The Macintosh changed everything. With its easy-to-use interface and relatively low price tag, the Macintosh made desktop publishing possible, and it proved to be immensely popular.

With the success of the Macintosh behind him, Jobs attempted to oust CEO John Sculley. The board of directors would not go along, and Steve Jobs resigned. He went on to found a company called NeXt. Rich Page went with him.

By 1996, Apple was in serious financial trouble, and unable to bring a new operating system to market. Instead, they went and got one from NeXt, and brought Steve Jobs on as an advisor.

In 1997, Steve Jobs was made interim CEO of what was then a $3 billion company. When he stepped down as no-longer-interim CEO in 2011, Apple was the most valuable consumer-facing brand in the world. In 2013, Apple became the most valuable company in history, with a market capitalization of $620 billion.

"There's no chance that the iPhone is going to get any significant market share. No chance."

— STEVE BALLMER,
MICROSOFT CEO, 2007

THE INTRODUCTION OF the Apple iPhone dramatically changed the cell phone business. Though other companies had attempted tepid forays into smartphones, none had come close to matching Apple's revolutionary product. Nearly 1.4 million iPhones were sold in the first three months.

In 2010, Microsoft followed suit and offered its own smartphone operating system. By 2014, Microsoft's platform had 3 percent of the smartphone market. Apple's had 42 percent.

In 1997, when Apple was barely hanging on as a company, Microsoft founder Bill Gates invested $150 million into the company. At the time Apple was worth less than $3 billion. Microsoft had a valuation in 2000 of $556 billion.

In 2012, Apple's iPhone generated more revenue than all of Microsoft's products combined. Steve Ballmer resigned as CEO in 2014.

"Dewey is in."

— POLLSTER ELMO ROPER, WHO QUIT TAKING SAMPLES ON SEPT. 9, TWO MONTHS BEFORE THE 1948 PRESIDENTIAL ELECTION

ONE OF THE landmark photos of the twentieth century is President Harry Truman holding up a *Chicago Tribune* that proclaims "Dewey Defeats Truman." Until late election night, that's exactly the result that was expected. Truman had not been a popular president and the Republicans had won control of both houses in 1946. Because of his low standing, several Democratic Party bosses began working to dump Truman.

Truman went on the attack, lambasting the "do-nothing" 80th Congress. He prevailed in getting the Democratic nomination and then turned his assault onto Dewey.

Truman toured much of the nation with his fiery rhetoric, playing to large, enthusiastic crowds. Still, a Dewey victory seemed guaranteed. The only person who appears to have considered Truman's campaign to be winnable was the president himself, who confidently predicted victory to anyone and everyone who would listen to him.

Truman outpolled Dewey by more than 2 million votes, and carried the electoral vote, 303 to 189, to win the election.

"The emotions of these painters (one of whom, Van Gogh, was a lunatic) are of no interest except to the student of pathology and the specialist in abnormality."

— *ROBERT ROSS, ART CRITIC FOR THE MORNING POST*

THOUGH HE PRODUCED more than 2,000 works, including 900 paintings and 1,100 drawings and sketches, Van Gogh sold only one painting, *The Red Vineyard*, during his ifetime.

After his death, memorial exhibitions were held in Brussels, Paris, The Hague, and Antwerp. In the early twentieth century, exhibitions of his work were held in Paris, Amsterdam, New York, and Cologne.

Today the Van Gogh Museum in Amsterdam is dedicated entirely to his work and the "crown jewel" of New York's Museum of Modern Art is his masterpiece *The Starry Night*.

In 1987, Van Gogh's *Irises* was sold for a record $53.9 million at Sotheby's New York. In 1990, his *Portrait of Doctor Gachet* was sold for $82.5 million at Christie's, thus establishing another record. Of the world's fifty most highly valued paintings, seven were created by Van Gogh, selling for a combined purchase price of better than $650 million.

"That damn Billy is not worth a Mississippi goddamn. Won't hold a job; won't try; won't do anything! He's a Falkner and I hate to say it about my own nephew, but hell, there's a black sheep in everybody's family and Billy's ours."

— *JOHN FALKNER*

THE FALKNER BLACK Sheep, known around Oxford, Mississippi, as "Count No-Count" because of his peculiar choice of attire, did have trouble holding down jobs. He could write, though.

From the early 1920s to the beginning of World War II, William Faulkner published thirteen novels and numerous short stories. Among these were the ground-breaking *The Sound and the Fury*, *As I Lay Dying*, *Absalom, Absalom!*, and *Light in August*. Ignored initially in his home country, Faulkner's reputation as a stylistic genius grew in Europe.

No one is sure why he changed his name from Falkner to Faulkner and he may not have been worth a Mississippi goddamn, but he was worth a Nobel Prize for Literature, which he received in 1949 for "his powerful and artistically unique contribution to the modern American novel."

"You can't sing a note or dance a step. You just don't have the talent."

— SEYMOUR LEBENGER, P.S.89 TEACHER, EXPLAINING WHY BARBARA STREISAND COULD NOT BE IN THE SCHOOL'S BIG FOLK-DANCE FESTIVAL

SHE MAY HAVE not made it into the folk-dance festival, but Barbara did okay. Originally wanting to be an actress, Streisand became a nightclub singer while still a teenager. In 1961, Orson Bean caught one of her shows at a Greenwich Village nightclub. He also happened to be a guest host on *The Tonight Show* and he booked Barbara for an appearance.

Dropping what she deemed an unnecessary "a," Barbra never looked back. In 1962, she first appeared on Broadway. Her first album won two Grammy Awards.

Since then Streisand has had a successful career in theater, film, and music. She has won Academy Awards for Best Actress and Best Original Song as well as multiple Emmy, Grammy, and Golden Globe awards.

"Kids imitate champions. If they try and imitate Fosbury, he will wipe out an entire generation of high jumpers because they will all have broken necks."

— PAYTON JORDAN, HEAD COACH OF THE 1968 UNITED STATES OLYMPIC TRACK TEAM

THE HIGH JUMP event requires that competitors only jump off one foot at takeoff — there is no rule addressing how a competitor crosses the bar, or how he or she lands. In the 1968 Olympics in Mexico City, every high jumper used the prevailing high jumping technique called the straddle. Except one.

Taking advantage of new soft cushioning that had replaced sand pits and enabled a competitor to land on his back, Dick Fosbury developed a bizarre-looking method where he approached the bar from an angle, and then jumped over the bar back-first, lifting both legs at the last instant. Universally derided by coaches and observers, Fosbury took his approach all the way to the 1968 Olympic Games.

Fosbury cleared 7'4" with the "Fosbury Flop," setting a new Olympic record and winning the gold medal.

By the 1972 Olympics, twenty-eight of forty high jumpers used the flop. The winner that year was Juri Tarmak, a straddler. It was the last time anyone using that technique won Olympic gold. The record high jump is 8' ½", set in 1993 by Javier Sotomayor. He flopped.

The straddle, though still a viable high-jumping method, is virtually obsolete.

"Groups of guitars are on the way out."

— DICK ROWE, DECCA RECORDS HEAD OF A&R, TO BEATLES MANAGER BRIAN EPSTEIN, 1962

DECCA RECORDS POLITELY turned down the Beatles. But then, so did HMV, Columbia, Pye, Philips, and Oriole. With his options running out, Epstein was able to secure an audition with Parlophone Records, an EMI susidiary label more famous for its comedy and novelty acts. Producer George Martin, feeling he had nothing to lose, signed the quartet.

Their initial single, "Love Me Do," peaked at a healthy number seventeen in the charts, and the follow-up, "Please Please Me," went straight to the top. Martin decided the band needed to cash in by releasing an album, which was recorded in one day. It went straight to number one, where it stayed for thirty weeks, only to be replaced by the group's second album, *With the Beatles.* By the end of 1963, Great Britain was engulfed in a national hysteria the press labeled "Beatlemania."

Dick Rowe, for his part, later made up for his error by taking some sage advice and signing the Rolling Stones to Decca. That advice came from Beatles guitarist George Harrison.

Fortunately, going forward, the Beatles would be dealing with shrewder and more sophisticated marketing folks.

"We don't think the Beatles will do anything in this market."

— ALAN LIVINGSTONE, PRESIDENT OF CAPITOL RECORDS, 1963

EVEN AFTER BEING signed by a sister label and trailblazing a year of unprecedented success in Britain, the Beatles still couldn't get the EMI American subsidiary, Capitol Records, to release their recordings in the United States.

A disk jockey in Washington, D.C., started playing "I Want to Hold Your Hand" and soon listeners were clamoring for it. The same thing happened in Chicago. Capitol wised up and released the song. A blitz marketing campaign culminated with the Beatles playing to a record 73 million television viewers on *The Ed Sullivan Show*. By April 1964, the Beatles held the top five spots in the *Billboard* singles chart and had released their first feature film, the highly acclaimed *A Hard Day's Night*.

The Beatles proceeded on to unheard-of fame, selling more than a billion records worldwide and revolutionizing how music was made in the studio. In *Rolling Stone's* "The 500 Greatest Albums of All Time," the Beatles hold three of the top five slots, four of the top ten, and five of the top fourteen. *Rolling Stone* declared, "The impact of The Beatles — not only on rock and roll but on Western culture — is simply incalculable."

Not bad for four kids who had no formal musical training and who had cut their teeth by playing eight hours a night in a red light district. Thankfully, during those formative times, they could always count on the support of family and friends.

"The guitar is all very well, John, but you'll never make a living at it."

— *MIMI SMITH, TO HER NEPHEW, JOHN LENNON*

JOHN LENNON WASN'T underestimated by just record executives — he got the same treatment at home.

Lennon was raised by his Aunt Mimi, a strict, no-nonsense type, and her opinion was well-intentioned. Yet despite his aunt's objection, Lennon kept playing the guitar and was able to eke out a living with the band that would evolve into the Beatles. For good measure, he went on to have a successful solo career after the band broke up.

At the time of Lennon's untimely death in 1980, his estate was valued at $235 million (equivalent to $720 million in 2015).

While he was with the Beatles, Lennon was noted for playing three guitars: the electric Rickenbacker 325 and Epiphone Casino, and the acoustic-electric Gibson J-160. Each one has now been issued in a John Lennon signature version.

“Who the hell wants to hear actors talk?”

— HARRY WARNER, CEO OF WARNER BROTHERS

WARNER'S QUOTE IS almost always taken out of context. When he said it, Warner Brothers was already heavily invested in marrying sound to moving pictures. Harry's full quote: "Who the hell wants to hear actors talk? The music — that's the big plus for us."

The motion picture industry at that time was the single largest employer of musicians, and the expense of paying thousands of theatre orchestras to play along with the pictures was more than substantial. By having a recorded soundtrack, Warner Brothers paid for the music once.

Nevertheless, Warner Brothers and the other studios had been very reluctant to adopt sound technology. Prior attempts before 1925 had made no inroads. Finally, Sam Warner, Harry's brother, was impressed enough with technology from Western Electric. The Vitaphone Corporation was created, and Sam was able to convince Harry to go forward.

Warner Brothers, though well-financed, was then a small studio that was losing money (in excess of $1.3 million for fiscal 1926). Two years later, the studio had released the first film with sound, *The Jazz Singer*, then followed that with others such as *Lights of New York* and *The Singing Fool*.

By 1929, Warner Brothers had a net profit of $14.5 million.

"The picture could have been speeded more at its beginnings, especially by the elimination of Dorothy's first song."

— ROBBIN COONS, ASSOCIATED PRESS, AFTER THE PREMIERE OF THE WIZARD OF OZ

"A needless delay in the story."

— HARRISON CARROLL, ENTERTAINMENT COLUMNIST FOR THE LOS ANGELES HERALD-EXPRESS

THE SONG IS often referred to as "Somewhere Over the Rainbow," but the actual title is simply "Over the Rainbow."

After a preview in San Bernardino, MGM execs felt the same way, and had the song removed from the film. But songwriters Harold Arlen and Yip Harburg fought to have it put back in, and after a fierce battle, it ultimately was.

The song is so popular that it topped the "Songs of the Century" list compiled by the Recording Industry Association of America and the National Endowment for the Arts.

"Stop it! There's nothing so useless on earth as knocking a string ball around a pasture with ruffians."

— PROFESSOR WILLIAM HERSCHEL COBB, TO HIS SON, TYRUS

THE "GEORGIA PEACH" set over ninety records during his career and is generally regarded as the greatest baseball player of his time. Though his marks for career hits and stolen bases have since been eclipsed, he still holds several records, including the highest career batting average (.366), a figure which is unlikely ever to be topped, and most career batting titles with twelve.

When Major League Baseball sent ballots out in 1936 to vote on the inaugural class for its Hall of Fame, five players were selected: Babe Ruth, Honus Wagner, Christy Mathewson, Walter Johnson, and Ty Cobb. Cobb tallied the highest vote total, having been named on 98 percent of the ballots. In 1998, the *Sporting News* ranked him as third on the list of 100 Greatest Baseball Players.

Cobb was also a skilled self-taught investor. Though the highest salary he ever received was $40,000, by the time he died in 1961, he was worth $12.1 million. With his fortune, he founded the still-thriving Ty Cobb Educational Foundation, which has assisted thousands of his fellow Georgians in attending college.

"Can't make a double-play, can't throw, can't hit left-handed, and can't run."

— SCOUTING REPORT ON PETE ROSE

BUT PETE ROSE can collect three batting titles, one Most Valuable Player Award, two Gold Gloves, the Rookie of the Year Award, compose a 44-game hitting streak, make seventeen All-Star teams, and play at least 500 games at five different positions. He can play on three World Champion teams and break Ty Cobb's record by finishing his career with 4,256 hits, the most in the history of Major League Baseball.

"We pass over the silly remarks of the President. For the credit of the nation we are willing that the veil of oblivion shall be dropped over them and that they shall be no more repeated or thought of."

— *EDITORIAL IN THE HARRISBURG PATRIOT AND UNION, NOVEMBER 14, 1863*

PRESIDENT LINCOLN'S REMARKS were part of a program dedicating the graveyard at Gettysburg, the scene of the great and pivotal Civil War battle fought four months prior. Preceding the president was Edward Everett, a statesman with an impressive political resume including senator, governor, and ambassador. By 1863, he was retired from politics, but as he was considered one of the greatest speakers of his day, he was asked to give the funeral oration.

Everett's speech took all of two hours to deliver. After a brief hymn, Lincoln made his dedication, which lasted all of two minutes.

In the century-and-a-half since it was delivered, it has remained among the most famous speeches in history. Virtually every schoolchild can recite its beginning: "Four score and seven years ago..."

On November 14, 2013, the *Patriot and Union* printed a retraction, stating they had failed to recognize the speech's "momentous importance, timeless eloquence, and lasting significance."

"Only in this time of soap bubble promotion could anybody take him seriously when he steps into the ring with Sonny Liston."

— *MILTON GROSS, ON CASSIUS CLAY'S FIRST TITLE FIGHT*

IN 1964, SONNY Liston was the World Heavyweight Champion. He had lost only once, and that was ten years prior. He won the championship in 1962 with a first round knockout of Floyd Patterson. Two more brutal first-round knockouts immediately preceded his fight with Cassius Clay.

Clay, on the other hand, was a trash-talking 22-year-old who had won the light-heavyweight gold medal at the 1960 Rome Olympics, displaying impressive hand and foot speed. However, he had been already knocked down twice in his short professional career, by Sonny Banks in 1962, and by Henry Cooper the following year. Few observers and fans gave him a chance against Liston. When time came for the fight, Clay was a seven-to-one betting underdog.

When the fight began, though, one thing became very clear: Liston couldn't hit Clay. Clay was simply too fast, and he landed combinations on Liston at will. Liston failed to answer the bell for the seventh round and Clay was World Champion. He later defeated Liston in a rematch, this time as Muhammad Ali.

"...such a man-made voyage will never occur regardless of all future advances."

— *LEE DE FOREST, 1957, ON TRAVELING TO THE MOON*

LEE DE FOREST was an inventor with more than 180 patents to his credit.

In 1906, De Forest invented the vacuum tube, thereby making amplification possible.

In 1907, De Forest became the first person to send a ship-to-shore radio message.

In 1910, De Forest was responsible for the first public radio broadcast.

In 1919, De Forest filed the first patent for a sound-on-film process.

In 1969, man landed on the moon.

"Björn Borg will never win Wimbledon with his style of tennis."

— *JACK KRAMER*

JACK KRAMER, A multi-winner at Wimbledon, should have had as good an idea as anyone regarding who could not win the world's premier tennis tournament on its famous grass surface. With Borg's unusual discus-throwing forehand and two-handed backhand hitting topspin-laden shots from the baseline, his style of play seemed more suited for slow clay surfaces.

But not only did Borg win at Wimbledon, he won the men's title five times in a row, an unheard of accomplishment, a record that had never been achieved since the prior year's champion had been required to compete in all the rounds (the record has since been equaled by Roger Federer).

Borg retired at the top of his game at the age of twenty-six with eleven career Grand Slam titles.

"We can well understand Ford management's wish to give the Mustang a distinctive or possibly unique appearance, but the results strike us as inexplicably amateurish...Better preparation for future improvement could hardly be devised."

— *CAR AND DRIVER MAGAZINE, ON FORD'S NEW CAR MODEL, 1964*

IN 1958, FORD Motor Company had rolled out the Edsel. Now infamous as one of the worst flops in automobile history, the model was stopped in 1960, with a loss to the company of more than $250 million. Understandably, Chairman and CEO Henry Ford II was apprehensive about launching a new, unproven line of cars.

Lee Iacocca, new general manager of the Ford division, was convinced that the coming-of-age baby boomers would create a market for what later became known as pony cars. After months of discussions and market surveys, Iacocca was able to convince the wary CEO and other executives. He got the go-ahead for the Mustang in September of 1962. An internal contest was held, and the winning design was chosen.

In April 1964, the Ford Mustang debuted at the World's Fair, and an intense marketing campaign followed.

The public disagreed with *Car and Driver.* Within eighteen months, 1 million Mustangs had been sold. By 2015, the Mustang was in its ninth generation, and the lines from the original design were still evident in the shape of the car.

"I have shown that the construction of an aërial vehicle which could carry even a single man from place to place at pleasure requires the discovery of some new metal or some new force. Even with such a discovery, we could not expect one to do more than carry its owner."

— *SIMON NEWCOMB, 1901*

NEWCOMB WAS AN astronomer and mathematician of some distinction, and his observation was included in a lengthy article he had written. In the article, he mentioned the absolutes of gravity and the luminiferous ether, the latter being a notion Einstein would soon leave in history's trash bin just four years later. But more importantly, Newcomb didn't grasp the concept of an airfoil, the mechanism that creates a pressure imbalance over and under a wing, enabling a plane to fly and a propeller to work.

No new metals and no new forces were discovered between 1901 and 1903, but on December 17 of that year, Orville and Wilbur Wright made the first sustained heavier-than-air flight.

Thirty years later, Boeing rolled out the 247, which was capable of carrying ten passengers.

"There'll never build 'em any bigger."

— CHARLES N. "MONTY" MONTEITH,
BOEING CHIEF ENGINEER,
AFTER THE FIRST FLIGHT OF THE
BOEING 247 TWIN-ENGINE PLANE
THAT HELD TEN PEOPLE, 1933

IN 1933, THE 247 was a fusion of innovation. The plane had cantilevered wings, retractable landing gear, a variable speed propeller, and a monocoque frame. Monteith was convinced that the 6.825 ton aircraft had reached the limits for structural safety.

Rival Douglas Aircraft Corporation promptly developed its DC-2 and DC-3, the latter holding thirty-two passengers.

Boeing's latest version of the 747, the 747-400, is slightly larger than the 247. Instead of ten, it can hold 416 passengers.

The double-decked Airbus A380 can hold 823 people in a one-class configuration.

"I thought the photography quite good, but nothing to write to Moscow about, the acting middling, and the whole thing a little dull...Mr. Welles' high-brow direction is of that super-clever order which prevents you from seeing what that which is being directed is all about."

— JAMES AGATE, CRITIC FOR THE SUNDAY TIMES, ON CITIZEN KANE

CITIZEN KANE, A film not-so-loosely based on the life of newspaper publisher William Randolph Hearst, was released in 1941 by RKO pictures. It promptly lost $150,000.

It may have not been a box-office success, but Orson Welles' directorial debut produced arguably the most important film in the history of cinema. Using a host of innovations in photography, sound editing, and dramatic structure, the 25-year-old Welles created a film that has gone on to inspire a multitude of filmmakers.

In 1997, and again in 2007, the American Film Institute placed *Citizen Kane* at number one on its list of the 100 greatest American movies of all time. In a recent poll of film critics and directors conducted by the British Film Institute, *Citizen Kane* was ranked the greatest film of all time.

"You are a car wreck."

— ATLANTA FALCONS HEAD COACH JERRY GLANVILLE, TO BRETT FAVRE

OVER GLANVILLE'S OBJECTIONS, Brett Favre was selected by the Atlanta Falcons in the second round, thirty-third overall, in the 1991 National Football League draft. Glanville's hesitancy appeared to be justified — Favre wasn't doing anything to impress the Falcons he was ready for the NFL. He was overweight and he missed team meetings. When he missed the team photo shoot, Favre told Glanville he was late because he was caught behind a car wreck, and Glanville responded with his terse opinion. Favre's first pass in an NFL regular season game was an interception returned for a touchdown. He only attempted four passes in his career at Atlanta, completing none.

Defying conventional logic and convinced of his talent, Green Bay Packers General Manager Ron Wolf traded a first-round draft pick to the Falcons for Favre during the following off-season. Favre became the Packers' starting quarterback in the fourth game of the 1992 season and subsequently led the Packers to seven division championships, two conference championships, and one Super Bowl victory. In the process, he won three consecutive Most Valuable Player Awards.

When he retired, his NFL records included most career passing yards, most career touchdown passes, and most career victories as a starting quarterback. His records for career passing yards and career touchdown passes have since been surpassed by Peyton Manning.

"Peyton Manning will likely never play football again, sources say"

— LOS ANGELES TIMES HEADLINE, JANUARY 2012

BETWEEN 1998 AND 2010, Peyton Manning passed for 54,828 yards and 399 touchdowns. He led the Colts to eight division championships, two conference championships, and one Super Bowl championship. He was named the National Football League's Most Valuable Player a record four times.

After experiencing neck pain and weakness in his arm, Manning opted for surgery in May 2011. Following the operation, he was unable to complete his throwing motion. Doctors advised he needed additional spinal fusion surgery and could not guarantee his return to the NFL.

He missed the 2011 season. Reports of his greatly diminished arm strength circulated, and speculation was rampant about the end of his career. Due to the uncertainty of his condition, the Colts released him in March 2012. Manning signed a contract with the Denver Broncos.

In 2012, he passed for 4,659 yards and was named NFL Comeback Player of the Year. In 2013, the Broncos scored an NFL record 606 points on their way to the Super Bowl. Manning set NFL marks with 5,477 passing yards and 55 touchdown passes. He was named the NFL's MVP for a record fifth time.

On February 7, 2016, he won his second championship when he led the underdog Broncos to a Super Bowl title over the Carolina Panthers.

"That's the worst idea I've ever heard. People hate spiders."

— MARTIN GOODMAN, TO STAN LEE

IN 1962, STAN Lee was doing pretty well. Having started a comic renaissance at *Marvel Comics* with the introduction of the Fantastic Four and the Incredible Hulk, Lee decided to pitch Spider-Man, a hero who possessed the powers of an arachnid, to Marvel publisher Martin Goodman.

Goodman's response was famously tepid, but when Stan Lee pointed out the character would be introduced in a comic they were cancelling anyway (*Amazing Adult Fantasy*), Goodman gave the go-ahead. The issue proved to be one of Marvel's highest-selling at the time, and *The Amazing Spider-Man* was quickly issued in 1963.

Spider-Man had begun his rise as a cultural icon. In addition to a plethora of comics and television shows, Spider-Man has been the star of five high-grossing films, as well as a Broadway show.

"News?...We don't need news. We counter-program against news. News loses money."

— *SID PIKE'S OPINION OF TED TURNER'S IDEA OF A 24-HOUR NEWS CHANNEL*

"Please Ted! Don't do this to us! If you commit to a venture of this size you'll sink the whole company!"

— *ANONYMOUS SIGN POSTED ON TED TURNER'S DESK*

BY THE END of the 1970s, Ted Turner had already amassed an enviable string of business successes. Taking over his father's billboard media business at age twenty-four, Turner turned it into the most successful business of its kind in the southeastern United States. He used the profits to buy radio stations. He also purchased Channel 17, a small UHF televison station, and convinced the FCC to allow him to broadcast the channel via satellite, thus giving birth to the superstation WTBS. The success of the Turner Broadcasting System allowed him to purchase both the Atlanta Braves and Atlanta Hawks.

In 1978, Turner had a new idea: a 24-hour news channel. The idea was hardly greeted with overwhelming support, but Turner, with the able assistance of Sid Pike, pressed on. After boldly stating, "We won't be signing off until the world ends," Turner launched CNN on June 1, 1980, with 25 staff members and 200 employees.

CNN revolutionized the industry. Instead of news being seen in a highly edited half-hour format, it could now be viewed as it happened, a fact that became very evident during its landmark coverage of the first Persian Gulf War.

A 2014 IPSOS Affluent Global Survey named CNN as the leading international news brand.

"Don't do that, Robert. You drive the people nuts. You can't play nothing."

— SON HOUSE, TO ROBERT JOHNSON, REGARDING JOHNSON'S IMPROMPTU GUITAR PLAYING

SON HOUSE WAS a well-respected Mississippi blues musician. Robert Johnson used to follow him around, much to Son's annoyance. Johnson himself wasn't a very good guitar player, but when he wasn't following Mr. House around, he was practicing and learning from other bluesmen. And then he got pretty good. In fact, he got so good that a legend started that he made a pact with the devil at a crossroads to sell his soul in return for being the greatest blues musician of all time.

His landmark recordings from 1936–1937 display an astonishing combination of singing, guitar skills, and songwriting talent that has influenced generations of musicians. Prominent on the album cover of Bob Dylan's groundbreaking *Bringing It All Back Home* is the Robert Johnson album *King of the Delta Blues Singers*. Johnson is often called the "Grandfather of Rock 'n' Roll." Eric Clapton simply called him "the most important blues singer who ever lived."

“42-1.”

*— ODDS AGAINST BUSTER DOUGLAS
DEFEATING MIKE TYSON
IN 1990 TITLE FIGHT*

ONLY ONE BETTING parlor in Las Vegas would offer odds for the 1990 Mike Tyson–Buster Douglas fight, as most everyone thought it was just an easy tune-up for the "unbeatable" Mike Tyson before a future bout with undefeated cruiserweight-champion-turned-heavyweight Evander Holyfield.

But Douglas had other ideas, dominating the fight from the beginning. Utilizing his twelve-inch reach advantage, he peppered Tyson with jabs and skillfully stayed out of range of Tyson's punches. Tyson finally unleashed his power in the eighth round, knocking Douglas to the canvas, but Douglas was able to beat the count easily.

In the tenth round, Douglas cut loose with a devastating combination, knocking Tyson down for the first time in Tyson's career. Tyson struggled up, awkwardly picking up his mouthpiece and putting it halfway back in his mouth. The referee stopped the fight.

"Mary Kay, liquidate the business right now and recoup whatever cash you can. If you don't, you'll end up penniless."

— ATTORNEY FOR MARY KAY HALLENBACK

"It's just a matter of time before the company goes bankrupt, and you along with it."

— ACCOUNTANT FOR MARY KAY HALLENBACK

UNHAPPY WITH BEING denied a promotion in favor of a man that she had trained, Mary Kay Rogers left her job in 1963 with the goal of writing a book to assist women in business. Instead of a book, she ended up with a business plan for her ideal company, which she promptly began planning with her new husband, George Hallenback.

One month into the marriage, and one month before the launch date, George died of a heart attack. Combining her life savings with those of her eldest son, and with her younger son taking her late husband's place, Mary Kay started Mary Kay Cosmetics. Using the principle of "praising people to success," she designed a business structure where advancement was predicated on helping others to succeed.

In 1963, she opened her first store in Dallas, Texas, with nine consultants. By the end of the year, the company had more than 300 consultants and sales of $198,000.

In 2012, Mary Kay Cosmetics had more than 2 million consultants and revenue in excess of $3 billion.

"I thought he simply couldn't run."

— "SUNNY JIM" FITZSIMMONS, FIRST TRAINER OF SEABISCUIT

SEABISCUIT FAILED TO win his first ten races. As a two-year-old, he raced an astronomical thirty-five times, coming in first five times and finishing second seven times. Most times, though, he was far back. The next racing season, the colt was again less than spectacular, and his owners sold him to automobile entrepreneur Charles S. Howard for $8,000.

His new trainer, Tom Smith, was successful where Fitzsimmons had not been. Paired with jockey Red Pollard, the horse finally hit his stride and became the star thoroughbred of the West Coast. Horse racing fans clamored for a race between "The Biscuit" and War Admiral, the 1937 Triple Crown winner.

On November 1, 1938, Seabiscuit met War Admiral in what was dubbed the "Match of the Century" at Pimlico Race Course. War Admiral was the prohibitive favorite (1-4 with most bookmakers) and a near unanimous selection of the writers and tipsters. In his greatest triumph, Seabiscuit went on to defeat War Admiral by four lengths.

After winning the Santa Anita Handicap in 1940, he was retired. A statue of him stands outside the Santa Anita Race Course.

"Television won't be able to hold onto any market it captures after the first six months. People will soon get tired of staring at a plywood box every night."

— *DARRYL ZANUCK, 1946*

DARRYL ZANUCK WAS an Academy Award-winning producer, a pillar of the old studio system, and one of the most important figures of the Golden Age of Hollywood.

As of 2010, there were more than 1.6 billion television sets in the world.

In the industrialized world, 98 percent of all homes have at least one television set.

In America and Europe, the average person watches television three hours and nine minutes a day.

"My doctors told me I would never walk again."

— *WILMA RUDOLPH*

THE TWENTIETH OF twenty-two children of Ed and Blanche Rudolph, Wilma Rudolph was born prematurely at four-and-a-half pounds. Over the next few years, she contracted measles, mumps, scarlet fever, chicken pox, and double pneumonia. When she was five, she was told she had polio. She was left with a paralyzed and useless left leg.

Blanche would not give up on Wilma. Having limited access to medical care in segregated Tennessee, she found out that Wilma could be treated at Meharry Hospital, a facility at a black medical college in Nashville. Even though it was fifty miles away, Blanche took Wilma there twice a week for two years. The doctors taught Blanche how to do physical therapy exercises at home. Finally, by age twelve, Wilma could walk normally, without crutches, braces, or corrective shoes.

Enjoying her new freedom, she joined the track team, where she was nicknamed "limpy Wilma" because she came in last in every race. One day she came in next-to-last.

On September 7, 1960, Wilma Rudolph became the first American woman to win three gold medals at the Olympic Games. She won the 100-meter dash, the 200-meter dash, and ran the anchor on the 400-meter relay team.

"I am certain that if you cannot prevent yourself from leading the idle, useless, unprofitable life you have had during your schooldays & later months, you will become a mere social wastrel…And you will degenerate into a shabby, unhappy, and futile existence."

— RANDOLPH CHURCHILL, IN A LETTER TO HIS SON, WINSTON

WINSTON CHURCHILL SERVED as President of the Board of Trade, Home Secretary, First Lord of the Admiralty, Minister of Munitions, Secretary of State for War, Secretary of State for Air, Chancellor of the Exchequer, Leader of the Conservative Party, and served two terms as Prime Minister.

His resolve during World War II made him an icon. He was awarded with orders and medals from the United Kingdom, the United States, France, Belgium, Denmark, Luxembourg, Spain, Nepal, Libya, Egypt, Norway, and the Netherlands.

In 1953, he was knighted and was also awarded the Nobel Prize for Literature.

In 1963, he was made the first Honorary Citizen of the United States.

When he died, he was given a state funeral, an honor normally only granted to royalty.

In a 2002 BBC poll of the 100 greatest Britons he was proclaimed "The Greatest of Them All."

"There seems to be too much cost involved for this kind of juvenile story. A risky story — one I would not do."

— INTERNAL MEMO TO UNITED ARTISTS HEAD MIKE MEDAVOY, OCTOBER 1975

AMERICAN GRAFFITI EARNED more than $55 million against a budget of $1.2 million, making it the most profitable film, percentage-wise, in motion picture history. Still, director George Lucas had a hard time convincing studio executives about his next film idea. At the time, science fiction wasn't a respected genre. Yet despite not having a book tie-in or any marketable stars attached, Fox finally went ahead and gave him the green light.

There was no applause at the initial screening — just silence. Even Lucas' wife called it "awful." The problem was Lucas had been so eager for a screening that he showed the film before the special effects were added in. Once that item was taken care of, it was screened again and the audience loved it.

Six months later, *Star Wars* was the highest grossing film of all time.

"Well, you'll be back in a few years."

— GEORGE LUCAS, SR., TO HIS SON GEORGE, JR., ABOUT HIS ULTIMATE RETURN TO THE FAMILY OFFICE SUPPLY BUSINESS

AFTER GEORGE REPLIED to his father by telling him he would be a millionaire by thirty, he co-founded American Zoetrope Studios with Francis Ford Coppola. Lucas then hit it big with the low-budget *American Graffiti* in 1973, and followed that up with *Star Wars*. In an inspired piece of negotiating, Lucas accepted a low director's fee in exchange for 40 percent of merchandizing rights to the *Star Wars* franchise.

In his spare time, he created a character named Indiana Jones with Steven Spielberg, designed the THX theatre sound system, and started Pixar Studios.

In 2013, *Forbes* estimated Lucas' personal wealth at $5.1 billion.

"He had a thin, sweet tone that was pretty bad. I would see him from time to time and each time there was some improvement but not enough to show much chance of him ever becoming more than an adequate musician."

— GENE RAYMEY, EARLY PEER OF CHARLIE PARKER

"You want to know about Charlie Parker? I'll tell you about Charlie Parker — he was lazy!"

— REBECCA RUFFIN, CHILDHOOD NEIGHBOR OF PARKER

PARKER MAY HAVE been lazy, but not when it came to his saxophone. He practiced the instrument diligently, up to fifteen hours a day. In 1939, he moved to New York to pursue a music career. He worked sporadically, but participated in many jam sessions.

During one of these jam sessions, he was playing "Cherokee," a piece with an unusual middle section of multiple musical keys. Not satisfied with the standard way of approaching a solo, he experimented with the melodic possibilities of the upper intervals of a chord, and making liberal use of the chromatic scale, unearthed a new realm of musical expression.

Parker played with contemporaries like Dizzy Gillespie, Thelonious Monk, and Kenny Clarke, first at Minton's Playhouse in Harlem, and later in the clubs of 52nd Street. Together they explored a more intricate and varied music, with complex harmonies and chord substitutions, unusual time signatures, and syncopation. Be-bop, as the new type of jazz became known, was radically different than the swing music that preceded it.

Parker changed jazz. Miles Davis summed it up this way: "You can tell the history of jazz in four words. Louis Armstrong. Charlie Parker."

"Mr. Berra...Frankly, and I say this for your own good, I don't think you can ever be a major league ballplayer. You're not built for this game."

— BRANCH RICKEY, ST. LOUIS CARDINALS GENERAL MANAGER

BRANCH RICKEY DIDN'T sign Yogi Berra. Instead, he signed Berra's neighbor, another catcher named Joe Garagiola.

When Yogi Berra retired, he held the American League records for catcher putouts and chances accepted. Known for his defensive prowess and excellent handling of pitchers, Berra played in more World Series games than any other player.

He won the Most Valuable Player Award three times, a feat accomplished by only three other players and no other catchers. According to sabermetrician Bill James, Berra is the greatest catcher of all time.

Rickey made up for his mistake by bringing Jackie Robinson to the Major Leagues.

"Unfortunately, [Jimmy Page] is also a very limited producer and a writer of weak, unimaginative songs, and the Zeppelin album suffers from his having both produced it and written most of it (alone or in combination with his accomplices in the group)."

— *ROLLING STONE'S REVIEW OF*
LED ZEPPELIN I, 1969

AFTER A SUCCESSFUL career as a session musician, Jimmy Page became a guitarist in the Yardbirds, the famous band that also claimed Eric Clapton and Jeff Beck as former members.

The Yardbirds disbanded in 1968, and left Jimmy Page with the rights to the name. He quickly reassembled a band, and after a brief incarnation as the New Yardbirds, the band adopted the moniker Led Zeppelin.

They released their eponymous first album in 1969. It was panned by the critics. The band toured extensively, and Jimmy Page kept writing songs and producing albums along with his accomplices.

Led Zeppelin went on to sell better than 300 million records.

As for the album, *Rolling Stone* apparently changed its mind. In 2012, the magazine ranked *Led Zeppelin* twenty-ninth on the magazine's list "The 500 Greatest Albums of All Time."

"These clodhoppers will not attack us, and should they do so, we will simply fall on them and rout them."

— COLONEL JOHANN RALL, HESSIAN COMMANDER AT TRENTON, 1776

LED BY GENERAL George Washington, the clodhoppers did indeed attack, surprising the mercenary Hessians after boldly crossing the icy Delaware River on Christmas night.

The Hessian forces suffered 22 fatalities, 83 serious injuries and 896 captures. The Americans suffered only 2 fatalities and 5 injuries.

The battle had an enormous impact on depleted American morale and kept the American Revolution alive.

"At least a third of the film is boring, needlessly and pathetically and uncondonably boring...That the character Snow White is a failure in every way is undisputable...Another Snow White will sound the Disney death-knell."

— V. F. CALVERTON, CRITIC
IN THE PUBLICATION
CURRENT HISTORY, 1938

WALT DISNEY HAD already dealt with his disappointments, declaring bankruptcy when starting out in Kansas City, and losing the majority of his staff in an unsuccessful dispute with Universal over a character called Oswald the Lucky Rabbit. But this did not stop Disney. In short order, he and his staff of animators made Mickey Mouse a household name and created the successful series *Silly Symphonies*. Then Disney decided he wanted to do a feature: *Snow White and the Seven Dwarves.*

This effort quickly became known around the film industry as "Disney's Folly." The prevailing opinion was the project would bankrupt the young Disney studio — no full-color animated feature had ever been done in English. Disney's relatives even tried to talk him out of it.

Beginning the technically-intense project in 1934, the studio ran out of money three years later. To acquire the funding to complete *Snow White*, Disney had to show a rough cut to Bank of America, which gave the studio the money to finish the picture. The finished film premiered in December 1937 and became the top grossing film of 1938. Disney was then able to build a new studio, and the Disney empire never looked back.

In 2006, Disney reacquired the rights to Oswald the Lucky Rabbit.

"I give the Stones another two years."

— *MICK JAGGER, 1963*

IN THE FIFTY-PLUS years since Jagger's prediction, the Rolling Stones have recorded and released twenty-two studio albums, eight concert albums, numerous compilations, and have sold more than 200 million albums worldwide.

In 2005, the Rolling Stones began the *A Bigger Bang* tour, which grossed more than $558 million. The tour lasted two years and sixteen days.

In February 2014, the Rolling Stones kicked off the *14 On Fire* tour. In May 2014, Mick Jagger became a great-grandfather.

“Victoria, I wish you’d quit saying that. That’s just not me. I’m not a preacher.”

— JOEL OSTEEN, TO HIS WIFE, VICTORIA

AT SOME POINT, someone at Lakewood Church was going to have to fill some big shoes. Lakewood's founder, John Osteen, had started the church in 1959, using a feed store as a meeting place for the congregation. In 1972, Lakewood grew to accommodate 500 members, and by 1987, 8,000 parishioners filled a new building.

Over the years, Osteen had tried to convince his son Joel to preach. Though ordained by the church in 1992, Joel had never done so. Having studied radio and televison communications in college, he preferred to work behind the scenes founding Lakewood's television program, where he produced his father's televised sermons for seventeen years.

With his father ill, Joel finally preached his first sermon on January 17, 1999. Within the week, John died of a heart attack.

Joel was a natural. Under his leadership, the church made the unprecedented move of leasing the former home of the Houston Rockets, the 16,800 seat Compaq Center, and converted it into their sanctuary. By 2010, the church owned the building.

Besides being the author of several best-selling books, Osteen's services are regularly attended by 43,000 church-goers, and are seen by more than 7 million broadcast media viewers weekly in more than 100 countries.

“How can we pitch you when you can’t get anyone out?”

— LOS ANGELES DODGERS GENERAL MANAGER BUZZIE BAVASI, TO SANDY KOUFAX’S COMPLAINT OF LACK OF PLAYING TIME

IN 1960, PITCHER Sandy Koufax asked Dodgers general manager Buzzie Bavasi to trade him because he wasn't getting enough playing time. Though he had a blistering fastball, Koufax struggled with control early in his career, and Bavasi was looking at a pitcher that had gone 36–40 since he had arrived in the majors five years before. Koufax actually was thinking about quitting baseball to devote himself to an electronics business that he'd invested in. Despite Koufax's request, Bavasi didn't trade him. After the last game of the season, Koufax threw his gloves and spikes into the trash.

After some soul searching, Koufax rededicated himself to the game and became the premier pitcher in baseball. From 1963–1966, he was more dominant than any pitcher ever, winning ninety-seven games while losing only twenty-seven. He was forced to retire at age thirty because of arthritis.

In his 12-season career, Koufax had a 165–87 record with a 2.76 ERA, 2,396 strikeouts, 137 complete games, and 40 shutouts. Throw in four no-hitters, one of which was a perfect game. He was the youngest man elected into the Hall of Fame at age thirty-six.

"John, I think we're going to have to drop Bob Dylan."

— COLUMBIA RECORDS EXECUTIVE, TO JOHN HAMMOND, 1963

IN FEBRUARY 1961, Bob Dylan began playing at various clubs around Greenwich Village. As fortune would have it, Dylan was asked to play harmonica for a Carolyn Hester album, and walked into the studio with a glowing review from Robert Shelton, critic for the *New York Times.* This got the attention of producer John Hammond — he signed Dylan immediately. Dylan recorded his first album in 1962 with only two original compositions. The album sold only 5,000 copies. Known around the Columbia offices as "Hammond's Folly," there was little enthusiasm for Mr. Dylan. Hammond, however, remained adamant.

Dylan's second album, *The Freewheelin' Bob Dylan,* justified Hammond's fervor. Dylan had discovered songwriting and spiced his sophomore effort with such classics as "Blowin' in the Wind," "A Hard Rain's A-Gonna Fall," and "Don't Think Twice, It's Alright." Soon entertainers everywhere were clamoring to cover his songs. Dylan then decided to "go electric" and delivered three of the most important albums in rock and roll history: *Bringing It All Back Home, Highway 61 Revisited* and *Blonde on Blonde.*

John Hammond went on to sign an unknown Bruce Springsteen. But this was par for the course for a man who was instrumental in the careers of Billie Holliday, Benny Goodman, Count Basie, Aretha Franklin, and Stevie Ray Vaughan. Besides John Hammond, another one of Dylan's biggest supporters was fellow Columbia artist Johnny Cash.

"That's going to keep you from making a living. You'll never do any good as long as you've got that music on your mind."

— RAY CASH, TO HIS SON, J.R.

IN A CAREER that spanned five decades, J.R. "Johnny" Cash crossed all sorts of musical genres: country, folk, blues, and rock and roll. His signature songs include "Folsom Prison Blues," "I Walk the Line," and "Ring of Fire."

Cash has been inducted into three major music halls of fame: the Nashville Songwriters Hall of Fame, the Country Music Hall of Fame, and the Rock and Roll Hall of Fame. He has sold more than 90 million albums.

Cash started his career at Memphis' Sun Records, the studio that also launched the careers of Howlin' Wolf, Jerry Lee Lewis, Carl Perkins, and Elvis Presley.

"You're never going to make it as a singer."

— EDDIE BOND, AFTER AUDITIONING THE YOUNG ELVIS PRESLEY FOR HIS BAND

"Well, it was alright, nothing out of the ordinary."

— BILL BLACK, ELVIS PRESLEY'S FIRST BASS PLAYER

ELVIS DIDN'T LET Eddie Bond's opinion of his audition keep him from moving forward. And Bill Black's first impression of Elvis Presley couldn't have been his last. Shortly after their initial 1954 meeting at Memphis' Sun Studios, "That's All Right" was released and quickly became a local sensation.

Within two years, Presley had signed with RCA and rock and roll had taken the country by storm. Presley's first *Ed Sullivan Show* appearance in 1956 was seen by 60 million viewers.

With his unusual gyrations, his sneer, and his magnificent voice, he soon became a cultural icon. He brought rock and roll music to the greater American public and influenced virtually every pop musician who followed in his wake.

His estimated worldwide record sales are greater than 1 billion.

“Don’t worry about that because no one is going to be watching anyway.”

— ESPN PROGRAMMING SCHEDULER TOM ODJAKJIAN, TO STEVE SABOL, 1980

AFTER BEING FIRED from his job in 1978 as communications director for the New England Whalers, Bill Rasmussen started ESPN with his son Scott and friend Ed Eagan.

The cable industry was in its infancy then — 24-hour programming had not been attempted yet, nor had anyone figured out how to tap the potential for advertising. Taking advantage of new satellite delivery systems, ESPN began presenting a little of everything to fill its broadcasting days: high school lacrosse, Australian rules football, tractor pulls, even the running of the bulls in Pamplona.

Around this time, Steve Sabol was gaining a small cult following by showing his video collection *NFL Films* around the country. Odjakjian, recently appointed scheduler of programming, approached him about showing the collection on the new channel, but only if Sabol would host the show. Sabol's apprehension prompted Odjakjian's reply.

Today ESPN reaches more than 100 million American households and delivers sports programming to sixty-one countries around the world.

"She is quite impossible to photograph. Too tall, too big-boned, too heavy all around. The face is too short, the mouth is too wide, the nose too long."

— CAMERAMAN, TO FILM PRODUCER CARLOS PONTI, REGARDING ACTRESS SOFIA LAZZARO

PRODUCER PONTI TALKED to the young actress about losing weight and getting a nose job. She did neither.

Lazzaro, after being renamed Sophia Loren, appeared in over ninety films. She won an Academy Award for Best Actress in 1960.

Apparently, Ponti was able to overcome Sophia's physical anomalies. He married the unphotographable woman, and per Italian law, committed bigamy in the process.

“I’m sorry, Mr. Kipling, but you just don’t know how to use the English language.”

— *EDITOR AT THE SAN FRANCISCO EXAMINER, TO RUDYARD KIPLING, 1889*

WITHIN TWO YEARS of this rejection, Rudyard Kipling had published a novel. Within eighteen years, he had been awarded the Nobel Prize in Literature.

At the award ceremony in December 1907, the Permanent Secretary of the Swedish Academy, C.D. af Wirsén, said, "The Swedish Academy, in awarding the Nobel Prize in Literature this year to Rudyard Kipling, desires to pay a tribute of homage to the literature of England, so rich in manifold glories, and to the greatest genius in the realm of narrative that that country has produced in our times."

"I heard a good rhythm section...go to waste behind the nihilistic excesses of two horns...They seem bent on pursuing an anachronistic course in their music that can be termed but anti-jazz."

— JOHN TYNAN, WRITER IN DOWNBEAT, AFTER SEEING JOHN COLTRANE AND HIS QUINTET PERFORM, 1961

BY THE TIME of Tynan's review, John Coltrane had already had a pretty good career. He had performed with Theolonious Monk and had played on Miles Davis' landmark albums, *Milestones* and *Kind of Blue.* In 1960, Coltrane started his own quartet, and in 1961, expanded it to a quintet when Eric Dolphy joined on second horn.

Using a then-considered-obsolete soprano saxophone, Coltrane and his quintet recorded *My Favorite Things* in October 1961, and followed that up with a legendary residency at the Village Vanguard in Greenwich Village a month later. During this time, his music was very experimental, influenced heavily by modal jazz and Indian ragas. Critics were fiercely divided in their estimation of Coltrane, and many audiences just simply didn't get it. Coltrane went on to record the landmark album *A Love Supreme.*

The influence of Coltrane spans many musical genres. He is the touchstone for virtually every post-1960 jazz saxophonist, and he has inspired an entire generation of jazz musicians. He was posthumously awarded the Grammy Lifetime Achievement Award in 1992 and received a Special Citation from the Pulitzer Prize Board in 2007 for "his masterful improvisation, supreme musicianship and iconic centrality to the history of jazz."

“That invention is practically worthless. It will never amount to anything.”

— WILLIAM ORTON, PRESIDENT OF WESTERN UNION, 1876

ALEXANDER GRAHAM BELL patented his telephone invention in 1876. He also taught deaf students, and two of his students' fathers, Gardiner Hubbard and Thomas Sanders, provided funds to start the Bell Telephone Company. But the company had trouble getting other investors. In attempting to do so, Hubbard pitched the invention to an attorney for a railroad company, Chauncey M. Depew. For a $10,000 investment, Depew would be awarded one-sixth of the patent.

The following day, Depew sought advice from William Orton, who was then president of the Western Union Telegraph Company. Hubbard gave his advice, and further pointed out that, on the off-chance the invention actually did amount to anything, Western Union already controlled the device due to a patent filed by Elisha Gray.

After finally realizing the invention's potential, Western Union went all out on the new technology using Gray's patent. The fledgling Bell Company filed suit against the giant. Bell won the patent dispute and, in 1885, became AT&T.

Depew would go on to serve in the U.S. Congress.

“I’m looking for Commander Bond and not an overgrown stunt-man.”

— IAN FLEMING, ON THE CASTING OF SEAN CONNERY AS JAMES BOND

APPROACHED BY HARRY Saltzman to bring his successful string of novels to the screen, Ian Fleming gave the producer a six-month option. That was all the time Saltzman needed. He formed EON Productions with co-producer Cubby Broccoli, procured financing with United Artists, and began work on *Dr. No*. But who was going to play the role of super-spy James Bond?

Fleming had named his spy after a man who had authored a book on birds, but had modeled Bond on several colleagues and, most notably, himself. He pictured Bond as a sophisticated Englishman and was considerably disappointed when the producers told him their choice to play Bond: Sean Connery.

Connery wasn't even English. He was a Scot and a former body builder with tattoos. Connery may have been a little rough around the edges, but he looked sharp in a tuxedo, and he brought a palpable edge and intensity to the character. Fleming liked Connery's portrayal so much he gave Bond a Scottish heritage in his next novel, *On Her Majesty's Secret Service.*

EON's James Bond franchise is one of the most successful in the history of motion pictures, taking in more than $6 billion, and it is still going strong over a half-century since the first film. Five other actors have played Bond during that time. A 2014 CBS News poll had respondents select who was the best. They selected Sean Connery, and it wasn't close.

“Maybe he can learn to lay carpet.”

— VICE PRINCIPAL, TO PAUL ORFALEA’S MOTHER, AFTER PAUL HAD FLUNKED OUT OF SCHOOL

“Don’t let him do that. He can’t even read.”

— PAUL’S AUNT CLAUDIA, SEEING HIM TRYING TO ASSEMBLE ORDERS AT THE FAMILY BUSINESS

PAUL ORFALEA FLUNKED second grade because he was unable to say his ABCs. In fact, he flunked out of four of the eight schools his parents enrolled him in. With the help of a tutor, he managed to graduate high school, eighth from the bottom of a class of 1,200 students. It turned out he had a disability that had not yet come into public attention: dyslexia.

In college, he was assigned to a study group to work on a class project, but since he couldn't read or write well, he ended up being the "gofer." That meant going to get coffee and making photocopies. Paul graduated, but due to his disability, he considered himself unemployable. So, he started his own company inside a 100-square-foot garage and charged for the use of the photocopier.

Paul Orfalea may not be a household name, but the company he started is: Kinko's. Purchased by FedEx in 2004, it has now been rebranded as FedEx Office with more than 1,700 locations in eleven countries, but people still call it Kinko's.

In 2001, the business school at California Polytechnic State University was named the Orfalea College of Business in his honor. The problem student went on to become visiting professor at the Global and International Studies Department of the University of California at Santa Barbara.

"It will be years — and not in my time — before a woman will lead a party or become Prime Minister."

— *MARGARET THATCHER, 1974*

MARGARET THATCHER BECAME leader of the Conservative Party in 1975.

She became Prime Minister of the United Kingdom in 1979.

She served in that position for the longest continuous period since Robert Jenkinson left the office in 1827.

“He hasn’t shown me much. He’s big, awkward, and doesn’t know what to do with himself.”

— TRAINER LUCIEN LAURIN, AFTER WATCHING SECRETARIAT GET BEAT BY FIFTEEN LENGTHS IN ONE OF HIS FIRST WORKOUTS

“There isn’t a standout horse in the field. This is not a good three-year-old year.”

— EDDIE ARCARO, TWO-TIME TRIPLE CROWN WINNING JOCKEY, BEFORE THE 1973 KENTUCKY DERBY

AS UNBELIEVABLE AS it sounds, the greatest racehorse of the modern era had to learn how to run. He struggled mightily at first, routinely getting embarrassed by other horses in workouts.

But when the colt got it together, he got it together in a big way. Finishing in front in all of his races except his initial one, he became the first two-year-old to be named Horse of the Year. Expectations were high, and there were rumors of the possibility of a Triple Crown winner, something that had not happened in twenty-five years.

After being syndicated for a then-record $6.08 million, Secretariat did not disappoint. He won the 1973 Kentucky Derby and Preakness in record times, and then, in what is universally regarded as the greatest performance by a modern race horse, demolished his Belmont Stakes field by thirty-one lengths, lowering the track record by the unheard-of 2 3/5 seconds. To this day, no other horse has come remotely close to his mark.

Incidentally, the horse that beat Secretariat in that workout was named Gold Bag, and was also entered in the 1973 Kentucky Derby. He finished eleventh. Finishing fourth was a gelding named Forego who, after Secretariat retired, won Horse of the Year three years in a row.

"It looks like the Gates of Hell. The region...is, of course, altogether valueless. Ours has been the first and will undoubtedly be the last, party of whites to visit the locality. It seems intended by nature that the Colorado River, along the greater portion of its lonely and majestic way, shall be forever unvisited and undisturbed."

— LT. JOSEPH IVES, AFTER VISITING THE GRAND CANYON, 1857

LIEUTENANT IVES HAD been asked by the United States War Department to lead an expedition to assess the feasibility of navigation from the Gulf of California. Ives and his party were the first of European descent to enter the canyon. They had quite a difficult time getting there, having to abandon their steamboat after it struck a rock.

Grand Canyon National Park attracts about 5 million visitors per year. Many of them are white.

"[The] theory of germs is a ridiculous fiction."

— FELIX-ARCHIMEDE POUCHET, 1865

LOUIS PASTEUR WAS conducting some experiments regarding beverage contamination and soon realized that fermentation was a process caused by the growth of microorganisms.

This observation led Pasteur to conclude that microorganisms infected animals and humans as well. He proposed preventing the entry of microorganisms into the human body. This put him at odds with Mssr. Pouchet, who favored the concept of spontaneous regeneration, where life manifested out of inanimate objects.

Although germ theory was highly controversial when first proposed, his ridiculous fiction is now a cornerstone of modern medicine and clinical microbiology.

Pasteur also created the first vaccine for rabies.

"...will be gone by June."

— VARIETY'S OPINION OF ROCK'N'ROLL, 1955

IN 1955, "ROCK Around the Clock" became the first rock and roll song to top *Billboard's* charts.

Fortunately for *Variety*, it didn't say June of what year.

"Four or five frigates will do the business without any military force."

— LORD NORTH, ON THE SIMMERING REBELLION IN BOSTON, 1774

IN THE 1770s, considerable friction existed between Great Britain and her American colonies. It took many forms, but the crux of the issue was this: the British Parliament asserted its right to tax the colonies, while many of the colonists steadfastly maintained that the right existed with its local governments. They objected to "taxation without representation," as no elected officers from the colonies served in Parliament.

After repealing the unpopular Stamp Act, Parliament stated its supreme authority by the Declaratory Act in 1766, and then came down hard on the colonies with the Townsend Acts, which were so loathed in the colonies that they were referred to as the "Intolerable Acts." Lord North led the Parliament to approve a partial repeal, but thought it a good idea to retain a tax on tea imports, a position further reiterated with the Tea Act of 1773.

Colonists responded by dumping 342 crates of tea into Boston Harbor. Lord North convinced Parliament to respond by passing the Boston Port Act. After that, the rest of the colonies got fired up and a continental congress was convened. The American Revolution was beginning.

North continued to serve as prime minister throughout the war. He tried to resign several times, but King George III would not accept his resignation. Finally, a year after the American victory at Yorktown, North stepped down for good.

"I'm going to get out of this business... The cinema is little more than a fad."

— *CHARLIE CHAPLIN, TO FELLOW COMEDIAN CHESTER CONKLIN*

OF COURSE, CHAPLIN did stay in the film business, and his early opinion of its future probably played a large part in how he negotiated his pay.

As for the cinema itself...

The first film shot in Hollywood was in 1910 by director D. W. Griffith. Soon an influx of other filmmakers followed to take advantage of the terrain and weather, favorable labor conditions, and especially to bypass the influence of the Motion Pictures Patent Company, Thomas Edison's east coast monopoly of film production and distribution. From those little acorns, an industry was born.

By 1920, 40 million people were going to the movies every week.

A century later, the global entertainment industry generates more than $2 trillion in annual revenue.

"Without the support of our organization, you'd be lost."

— *MACK SENNETT, TO CHARLIE CHAPLIN*

IN 1912, MACK Sennett founded Keystone Studios, famous for the Keystone Cops. After seeing Charlie Chaplin on a vaudeville tour, Sennett hired him for $1,500 a week.

In the film *Kid Auto Races at Venice*, Chaplin introduced a character that would become an icon: The Tramp. By 1914, Chaplin was making a film a week. With his success, he asked for a raise, prompting Sennett's response. Chaplin left Sennett and Keystone.

Within two years, Chaplin was internationally famous and was making $10,000 a week (equivalent to $235,000 in 2015). Aware of his value and once again dissatisfied with his income, Chaplin, along with Mary Pickford, Douglas Fairbanks and D. W. Griffith, formed their own distribution company, United Artists.

In 1972, the Academy of Motion Picture Arts and Sciences presented Chaplin an honorary Oscar for "the incalculable effect he has had in making motion pictures the art form of this century."

He was greeted with a 12-minute standing ovation.

"Ruth made a great mistake when he gave up pitching. Working once a week he might have lasted a long time and become a great star."

— TRIS SPEAKER, BASEBALL HALL OF FAMER, TALKING ABOUT BABE RUTH, 1921

TRIS SPEAKER WAS the greatest center fielder of his time and one of the first five men inducted into the National Baseball Hall of Fame, so he should have known what he was talking about.

He didn't.

Despite his exceptional pitching numbers, Ruth's hitting prowess had become more than obvious. He batted better than .300 in both 1917 and 1918. During the 1919 season, Ruth threw a pitch in only seventeen games. He also set the Major League home run record that year with twenty-nine. He broke that the next year with fifty-four, and the next with fifty-nine.

By the time he retired, the Sultan of Swat had hit 714 home runs, held a .342 lifetime batting average, and still holds the record for the highest career slugging percentage (.690). No one else is close.

Baseball statistician extraordinaire Bill James called him the greatest all-around player in the history of baseball.

"If ever I saw a cover picture for the snob magazines, she's it."

— JACK OLIPHANT, AFTER VIEWING AUDREY HEPBURN IN 1950

"Yes, she's pretty, but dumb."

— CECIL LANDEAU'S RESPONSE

AUDREY HEPBURN WAS just dumb enough to win an Academy Award for Best Actress in her first starring role in *Roman Holiday*. She was also just dumb enough to win a Tony, a Grammy, an Emmy, and a Golden Globe.

Further utilizing her inherent dullness in the midst of one of Hollywood's most successful acting careers, she somehow managed to become the style and fashion icon of the 1950s.

Shortly after Hepburn's final film role, the snob, who had suffered malnutrition while growing up under Nazi occupation in her native Holland, was appointed a Goodwill Ambassador of UNICEF, and dedicated the remainder of her life to helping impoverished children throughout the world.

“The die-hard, the pro-foreign advocates have been especially loud in their derision of the new car.”

— *ROAD & TRACK MAGAZINE, 1953*

AND WHY WOULDN'T they?

The new car handled poorly, it rattled, its brakes weren't any good, and it had a two-speed transmission, which isn't exactly ideal for a sports car. On top of that, it had three carburetors that needed tuning and aerodynamics so sub-standard that exhaust was sucked forward, thereby staining the paint.

Such was the auspicious debut of the Chevrolet Corvette. And sales followed accordingly. Projected second year sales were 12,000, but by the end of 1954, only 3,640 had been produced.

By 1956, Chevrolet had made massive improvements to the car, installing a V8 engine, thereby increasing horsepower from 115 to 210 BHP (225 with optional twin barrels), and equipping it with a three-speed manual transmission.

Sales hit five figures by 1960, and three years later when Chevrolet introduced the Sting Ray version, the car achieved icon status.

As of 2016, the Corvette is in its seventh generation of production.

"Although it may be admirably suited for a few specialized copying applications, the Model 914 has no future in the office-copying-equipment market."

— *ARTHUR D. LITTLE'S 1958 MARKETING ANALYSIS OF XEROX'S FIRST COMMERCIAL COPIER*

THE HALOID COMPANY was founded in 1906 in Rochester, New York, and originally manufactured photographic paper and equipment. In 1947, it took interest in xerography, a photocopying process that had been invented by Chester Carlson a decade before. Carlson's invention required yet another decade of development until the company finally felt ready to move forward with the introduction of the first plain paper photocopier, the 914, and eagerly sought business partners with some clout to bring the machine to market.

Mighty Kodak said no, as did others. And upon the analysis by A.D. Little that estimated a market of no more than 5,000 customers, IBM decided against it. Haloid had no choice but to go forward by itself. Instead of just trying to sell the 914, as A. D. Little assumed, the company opted to also lease the machine. By the end of 1962, Haloid was Xerox and took in almost $176 million in revenue.

The A.D. Little estimate of 5,000 proved to be slightly off. Seven years after its introduction, Xerox had placed 190,000 copiers into businesses.

In 2013, Xerox had revenues of better than $21 billion.

"He looks about three feet tall, so dead serious, so humorless, so unkempt. This is going to be a disaster."

— *KATHERINE ROSS, ON*
THE GRADUATE CO-STAR
DUSTIN HOFFMAN

"You know, when he first came in, I thought he was one of the messenger boys."

— *PRODUCER JOSEPH E. LEVINE*

PER CHARLES WEBB'S novel, Benjamin Braddock was blonde and bronzed, like Robert Redford, who wanted the part, and who had already worked for director Mike Nichols in Broadway's *Barefoot in the Park*. But in one of the most famous examples of across-the-grain casting, Nichols hired Dustin Hoffman.

The Graduate became a cultural phenomenon, earning $35 million in its first six months, and Hoffman received an Academy Award nomination for his performance.

Hoffman went on to become one of the most celebrated actors of his time, having been nominated seven times for the Academy Award for Best Actor and taking home the trophy twice.

"He hasn't seen defenses like ours in his league."

— BALTIMORE COLTS DEFENSIVE END BILLY RAY SMITH, ON JOE NAMATH, BEFORE SUPER BOWL III

BILLY RAY SMITH'S statement was in response to Joe Namath's famous boastful guarantee that the New York Jets would win Super Bowl III. And the evidence was all on Smith's side. The Colts' defense led the National Football League in fewest points allowed and ranked third in total rushing yards allowed. Defensive end Bubba Smith was considered the NFL's best pass rusher, and Mike Curtis was thought to be the top linebacker in the league. After winning the 1968 NFL title, the Colts were touted by the sports media as "the greatest team in pro football history."

The Jets were not near as dominant, and represented the American Football League, whose teams had been utterly dominated in the first two Super Bowls. The Jets were made 18-point underdogs.

Joe Namath completed 17 out of 28 passes for 206 yards, and was named the game's Most Valuable Player. The Jets, from the "inferior" AFL, won 16–7.

"...In a short time it was demonstrated that the instruments as manufactured had little or no practical or commercial value."

— *THOMAS EDISON, IN AN 1894 AFFIDAVIT, REGARDING THE PHONOGRAPH*

EDISON'S PHONOGRAPH AND its first commercial rival, the graphophone, were not overly successful, probably because they were marketed as office dictation machines.

In 1895, Emile Berliner introduced a commercial version of the record player he had been developing for eight years. The player used a rotating disc instead of a cylinder and was dubbed the gramophone. The best part was that the discs could be mass-produced very easily. The speed at which the disks were rotated was eventually standardized at 78 rpm. Later innovations allowed lower rotations: 45 and 33 1/3 rpm. Very quickly there appeared a mass market for popular recording, and an industry was born.

One of the world's most famous trademarks is a dog listening to "His Master's Voice" on a gramophone. It was acquired from the English artist Francis Baraud in 1899 by the newly-formed Gramophone Company, later to become HMV, then RCA Victor.

The dog's name was Nipper.

"Fooling around with alternating current is just a waste of time. Nobody will use it, ever."

— *THOMAS EDISON, 1889*

DURING THE INITIAL years of electricity distribution, Thomas Edison was aggressively promoting direct current as a standard. Direct current worked well with incandescent lamps, which Edison had invented, and it also worked well with electric motors.

Nikola Tesla, who had once worked for Edison, had a different idea. Alternating current, an electric current that reverses direction cyclically, could be transmitted over long distances at high voltages, thus requiring less power sources. When Tesla, partnered with George Westinghouse, introduced a system for alternating current generators, transformers, motors, wires and lights in 1887, it became clear that alternating current was a superior and more efficient way of transmitting electricity.

Edison, on the verge of losing a lot of money from patent royalties and the construction of power plants, carried out a vigorous campaign against alternating current, including publicly killing horses and elephants.

This time the Wizard of Menlo Park was wrong. Tesla and Westinghouse won the international Niagara Falls Commission contract in 1893.

Alternating current is the electrical standard worldwide.

"The proposition that the Earth is not the center of the world, nor immovable, but that it moves, and also with a diurnal motion, is also absurd and false philosophically, and, theologically considered, at least erroneous in faith."

— CATHOLIC CHURCH, IN ITS SENTENCING OF GALILEO, 1633

IN THE SIXTEENTH century, the prevailing view of the cosmos was one put forth by Ptolemy 1,400 years prior — that the Earth was at the center of the universe and the heavens revolved around it.

Nicolas Copernicus, an astronomer and a Catholic clergyman, decided the evidence showed that the earth revolved around the sun. His formal theory was announced in *De revolutionibus orbium coelestium*, just before his death in 1543. Initially, it only provoked mild controversy, but within sixty years, a considerable backlash had developed.

In 1616, Galileo Galilei, the inventor of the telescope and a follower of the Copernican theory, was made to appear before a Catholic tribunal. In 1633, he was brought forth again and received the famous papal condemnation.

Lest history judge the Catholic Church too harshly, it should be noted that the *Commentariolus*, an early outline of Copernicus' theory, was disparaged by the Protestant reformer Martin Luther. Scriptural interpretations aside, their reactionary approach was understandable. After all, the Earth doesn't feel like it moves. When Isaac Newton published his *Philosophiæ Naturalis Principia Mathematica* in 1687, explaining the laws of motion and universal gravitation, the heliocentric view held sway.

“Men might as well project a voyage to the Moon as attempt to employ steam navigation against the stormy North Atlantic Ocean.”

*— DR. DIONYSIUS LARDNER,
PROFESSOR OF NATURAL PHILOSOPHY
AND ASTRONOMY, UNIVERSITY
COLLEGE, LONDON, 1838*

DIONYSIUS LARDNER WAS a prominent scientific lecturer and author of *The Steam Engine Explained and Illustrated.*

Despite his prediction, regularly scheduled trans-Atlantic crossings began that very year with the paddle steamer *SS Great Western.* And despite Mr. Lardner's calculations, the ship was more than able to carry enough coal for its journey.

Man landed on the moon in 1969. The Saturn V rocket did not require coal.

“Professor Goddard does not know the relation between action and reaction and the need to have something better than a vacuum against which to react. He seems to lack the basic knowledge ladled out daily in high schools.”

—JANUARY 13, 1920 NEW YORK TIMES EDITORIAL ABOUT ROBERT GODDARD'S ROCKET WORK

IN 1919, THE Smithsonian Institution published Goddard's work, *A Method of Reaching Extreme Altitudes.* The book described Goddard's mathematical theories of rocket flight, his experiments with solid-fuel rockets, and the possibilities that rockets brought.

The publication gained him national attention, most of it negative. Although Goddard's point of targeting the moon was only a small part of the work and intended as an illustration of possibilities, newspapers sensationalized his ideas. On January 13, 1920, an unsigned *New York Times* editorial took almost perverse delight in heaping scorn on the concept.

On July 17, 1969, the day after the launch of Apollo 11, the mission that would land on the moon, the *New York Times* published an item entitled "A Correction." It summarized the 1920 editorial mocking Goddard, and then concluded, "Further investigation and experimentation have confirmed the findings of Isaac Newton in the 17th century and it is now definitely established that a rocket can function in a vacuum as well as in an atmosphere. The Times regrets the error."

“Can’t act. Slightly bald. Can dance a little.”

— *RESPONSE TO FRED ASTAIRE’S MGM SCREEN TEST*

BY THE TIME this comment was made, Fred Astaire had already begun a successful dancing career on Broadway. The test was a disappointment, but David O. Selznick, who had commissioned it, stated in a memo, "I am uncertain about the man, but I feel, in spite of his enormous ears and bad chin line, that his charm is so tremendous that it comes through even on this wretched test."

Astaire made his film debut dancing with Joan Crawford in *Dancing Lady*. His next film was with a young lady named Ginger Rogers, with whom he made nine more films.

His stage and film career lasted seventy-six years. In 1999, the American Film Institute named him the fifth Greatest Male Star of All Time. Rudolph Nureyev rated him as "simply the greatest, most imaginative dancer of our time."

"Forget it, Louis, no Civil War picture ever made a nickel."

— IRVING THALBERG, TO MGM HEAD LOUIS B. MAYER, REGARDING GONE WITH THE WIND

IRVING THALBERG WAS known as "The Boy Wonder." By the age of twenty-one, he already was an executive in charge of production. He was famous for his extraordinary ability to select the right scripts, the right actors, the best production staffs, and make very profitable films.

As far as *Gone with the Wind*, David O. Selznick felt differently. The producer's tenacity in getting the best-selling novel to screen has become the stuff of legend, even inspiring a movie about his effort.

Upon its release, *Gone with the Wind* had a domestic gross of $198,676,459. Adjusted for inflation, it is the highest-grossing film of all time.

“I’m afraid he’s just a big, stiff running back.”

— VINCE DOOLEY, GEORGIA BULLDOGS HEAD COACH, AFTER WATCHING PRIZE RECRUIT HERSCHEL WALKER IN PRACTICE, 1980

IN 1979, RECRUITERS from all major colleges descended on Wrightsville, Georgia. They were after Herschel Walker, who was a 6'2", 220-pound running back with world-class speed. In his senior year, Walker led Johnson County High School to its first state championship by rushing for 3,167 yards. When all offers were in, Walker chose the University of Georgia.

After watching Walker struggle in a few practices, Coach Dooley made his assessment, and subsequently, Walker started the season as the third-string tailback. With Georgia trailing Tennessee 15–2 and his offense doing nothing, Dooley put in Walker, who promptly ran over All-SEC safety Bill Bates for a touchdown. Later Walker scored again and Georgia won 16–15.

It was Georgia's first victory of an undefeated national championship season. Walker finished with 1,616 yards, a freshman record, and placed third in the Heisman Trophy balloting. Playing only three years, he set 10 NCAA records, 15 Southeastern Conference records, 30 Georgia records, and won the 1982 Heisman Trophy. He then went on to have an outstanding professional career in two leagues.

In 1999, he was selected to *Sports Illustrated*'s NCAA Football All-Century Team. Fox Sports Net named Walker the best college football running back of all time.

"A little slack, a little soft, more than a little artificial, 'The Great Gatsby' falls into the class of negligible novels."

— *THE SPRINGFIELD REPUBLICAN, 1925*

UNLIKE F. SCOTT Fitzgerald's first two novels, *This Side of Paradise* and *The Beautiful and Damned, The Great Gatsby* was not successful upon its release. The book went through two printings totaling 23,870 copies. When Fitzgerald died in 1940, he was an alcoholic screenwriter in Hollywood who had been largely forgotten. Obituaries used *Gatsby* as evidence of the great potential never reached.

After its republishing in 1945 and 1953, the novel had a rebirth of interest. It has since become a standard text in high school and university courses on American literature in countries around the world. It is ranked number two in the *Modern Library's* list of the 100 best novels of the twentieth century, second only to James Joyce's *Ulysses*.

"An illiterate, underbred book it seems to me...ultimately nauseating."

— *VIRGINIA WOOLF, ON JAMES JOYCE'S ULYSSES, 1922*

WOLFE WENT ON to describe Joyce's novel as diffuse, brackish, and pretentious.

Ulysses chronicled the passage through Dublin by its main character, Leopold Bloom, during an ordinary day, June 16, 1904. Structured on the ancient work *The Odyssey*, it isn't the easiest read as Joyce uses a non-linear, stream-of-consciousness technique and experimental prose.

In mild contrast to the opinion of Ms. Woolf, the *Modern Library* in 1999 ranked *Ulysses* first on its list of the 100 best novels of the twentieth century.

"Whom could this operetta offend? Only those of us who, despite the fact that we may respond, loathe being manipulated in this way and are aware of how cheap and ready-made are the responses we are made to feel. We may become even more aware of the way we have been turned into emotional and aesthetic imbeciles when we hear ourselves humming the sickly, goody-goody songs."

— PAULINE KAEL'S REVIEW OF THE SOUND OF MUSIC

IN HER TIME, Pauline Kael was arguably the most influential entertainment critic there was.

The Sound of Music offended a good number of emotional and aesthetic imbeciles. Adjusted for ticket price inflation, it is the third highest-grossing film of all time, behind only *Gone with the Wind* and *Star Wars*.

In 2007, Twentieth Century Fox conducted a poll for the greatest musical of all time and ranked *The Sound of Music* number one.

"It's not possible."

— PAUL KOECHLI, FORMER COACH OF GREG LEMOND, ON CATCHING LAURENT FIGNON IN THE 1989 TOUR DE FRANCE

IN 1986, GREG LeMond became the first American to win cycling's premier event, the Tour de France, defeating teammate and five-time champion Bernard Hinault.

The following year, he was accidentally shot by his brother-in-law in a freak hunting accident. An operation saved his life, but LeMond was left with thirty shotgun pellets still in his body (two in the lining of his heart). Despite that, LeMond was determined to return to racing, but struggled through 1988 and the early part of 1989.

Still working his way into condition by the time of the '89 Tour, he was not considered a favorite for the race. But LeMond got off to a great start, and over the next few days, he and two-time winner Laurent Fignon battled for the lead. When Fignon dominated the next to last stage in the Alps, LeMond was fifty seconds behind going into the final 24.5 kilometer time trial stage. By cycling standards, those fifty seconds were a virtual eternity, and Fignon was universally thought a lock to win. Fignon even stated LeMond's catching him was "impossible."

LeMond bettered Fignon's time by almost a full minute, winning the Tour by eight seconds.

For good measure, he won the Tour again in 1990.

“Of all the students in the class, he showed the least promise because he seemed to have less equipment than anybody else.”

— NORMAN ROSE, GUEST ACTOR AT ACTORS STUDIO, AFTER SEEING MARLON BRANDO IN A DRAMATIC WORKSHOP, 1943

WITHIN A YEAR of this observation, Marlon Brando had debuted on Broadway in *I Remember Mama*. Critics voted him "Broadway's Most Promising Actor" for his role in *Truckline Café*, although the play only had thirteen performances before it was cancelled. In 1947, Brando achieved stardom as Stanley Kowalski in Tennessee Williams' play, *A Streetcar Named Desire*, directed by Elia Kazan.

Brando's performance revolutionized acting, popularizing the Stanislavski "method," an internalized approach to character which contrasted sharply with classical acting.

Brando won the Academy Award for Best Actor in a Leading Role for his performance in *On the Waterfront* in 1954.

"No! No! Absolutely not, I don't want a crazy guy!"

— *CHARLES BLUHDORN, GULF+WESTERN CEO*

IN 1949, CHARLES Bluhdorn started a company that became Gulf+Western, and in 1966, that company purchased Paramount Pictures. Not a hands-off managerial type, Bluhdorn took an active role in the decisions that were made at the studio.

Paramount hired Francis Ford Coppola, fresh off an Oscar win for Best Screenplay for *Patton*, to direct a film about the mafia entitled *The Godfather*. Coppola and Paramount executives were soon tangling over the casting. Coppola wanted Marlon Brando to play the lead role of Don Corleone, while Paramount executives were adamant that he not have it. Brando, widely considered the greatest actor of his generation, had fallen into disfavor in Hollywood because of working habits, lack of recent box-office success, and support of various controversial causes.

Frustrated, Coppola made a screen test of Brando and took a copy straight to the top man in New York. Bluhdorn's immediate reaction was adamantly against, but by the end of the screen test, he was sold.

The Godfather won the Academy Award for Best Picture of 1972. Marlon Brando won his second Academy Award for Best Actor in a Leading Role.

"The music...is a full-fledged attack on the ears and on the brain. Using devices such as controlled feedback and a shrieking viola, the Velvet Underground attacks, grates, screams, and pounds on the eardrums until the mind is virtually reduced to oatmeal."

— TIMOTHY JACOBS' REVIEW OF THE VELVET UNDERGROUND AND NICO, 1967

JACOB'S REVIEW WAS actually one of the more positive reviews of the Velvet Underground's debut effort. The album was released in March 1967, making it to the exalted spot of #171 on *Billboard's* Top 200 chart.

By 1973, the band was finished, having had virtually no commercial success. Yet the Velvet Underground is one of the most important and influential rock and roll groups of all time. Music producer Brian Eno famously quipped that, although the group didn't sell many records in its lifetime, everyone who bought one went out and started a band. Critic Lester Bangs said, "Modern music begins with the Velvets and the implications of what they did seem to go on forever."

In April 2003, *Spin* ranked *The Velvet Underground and Nico* at the number one spot on their "Top Fifteen Most Influential Albums of All Time" list, and in November of the same year, *Rolling Stone* placed it at number thirteen on their list of "The 500 Greatest Albums of All Time." In 2006, *Uncut* ranked it number one on its list of "100 Greatest Debut Albums."

"We cannot accept his 'Sunday at La Grande Jatte' for the tones in this painting are crude and the figures are set against the light in a way that makes them resemble poorly articulated wax figures."

— EMILE HENNEGUIN, ART CRITIC IN LA VIE MODERNE, 1884

WHEN GEORGES SEURAT presented his giant canvas *Un Dimanche a la Grande Jatte* at the Eighth Impressionist Exhibition in Paris in 1884, the reviews were hardly warm. After all, what was one to make of a painting composed entirely of colored dots?

Seurat had just spent two years on the work, pioneering a technique which became known as pointillism (at first derisively), in which small distinct points of primary colors create the impression of a wide selection of secondary and intermediate colors.

Five years after the exhibition, Seurat was dead, but his painting had changed art, paving the way for artists like Van Gogh and other post-impressionists.

La Grande Jatte is now the prized possession of the Art Institute of Chicago.

“The most insipid, ridiculous play that I ever saw in my life.”

— SAMUEL PEPYS’ DIARY ENTRY, SEPTEMBER 29, 1662

SAMUEL PEPYS WAS a member of the British Parliament and served as Secretary of the Admiralty, but is most famous for a detailed private diary he kept during 1660–1669, which is now one of the most important sources for studying the English Restoration period.

The play Pepys was referring to: *A Midsummer Night's Dream* by one William Shakespeare.

The English went through a period in the 1700s now referred to as the English Interregnum. During this reactionary period, "drama" was banned and all theatres were closed from 1642–1660. When the theatres reopened, *A Midsummer Night's Dream* reappeared, as did many other Shakespearean plays. It was after one of these performances that Pepys passed his immortal judgment.

The comedy has since been performed on countless occasions around the world, but yet was unable to escape Mr. Pepys' ire. Thankfully, Mr. Shakespeare is more renowned for his tragedies.

"It is a rude and barbarous piece... one might suppose such a work to be the fruit of the imagination of a drunken savage."

— *VOLTAIRE, 1748*

FRANÇOIS-MARIE AROUET, better known by the nom-de-plume Voltaire, was a French Enlightenment writer and philosopher known for his caustic wit and defense of civil liberties. He was a prolific writer, producing works in almost every literary form. In his *Dissertation sur la tragédie ancienne et moderne*, he made mention of an English author and a certain play.

The author: William Shakespeare. The play: *Hamlet*.

Voltaire did acknowledge that *Hamlet* contained "sublime strokes worthy of the loftiest geniuses," but in a correspondence to fellow playwright Bernard Joseph Saurin, Voltaire again called Shakespeare a savage and maintained that *Hamlet* could only be popular in England and Canada.

During Shakespeare's lifetime, the vulgar, barbarous piece was one of his most popular works performed in The Globe Theatre. Four hundred years later, it still is among the most performed around the globe, even outside of England and Canada.

No empirical evidence exists for or against Mr. Shakespeare's being drunk when he wrote *Hamlet*.

"Monstrous...tasteless, and in its handling of Schiller's Ode, so trivial."

— LUDWIG SPAHN, UPON HEARING BEETHOVEN'S NINTH SYMPHONY

NOT ALL WERE impressed with Ludwig von Beethoven's *Symphony No. 9 in D minor.* Beethoven now stands as a cultural pillar, but at the time his music was often perceived as aggressive and dissonant, very different from what listeners had become accustomed to from giants like Haydn and Mozart.

Beethoven, as always, was "pushing the envelope." His *Ninth* was the first symphony to make use of the human voice. It was also Beethoven's last, and found him at the apex of his talent. In time, audiences adjusted, and the brilliant symphony's popularity continued to grow. In Western culture, the *Ninth* is now ubiquitous, and the *Ode to Joy* from the symphony's fourth movement, a musical adaptation of Friedrich Schiller's poem, has been heard by virtually everyone.

One person who did not hear it was Beethoven himself. By the time he composed the symphony, he was completely deaf.

Afterword

THIS IS NOT a large or complicated book, but it did require a surprising amount of research. I spent a good swath of time in the public libraries in Dallas, Portland, and Savannah. I owe special thanks to Barnes & Noble, Half-Price Books, and Portland's (and the world's) greatest book store, Powell's Books, for not kicking me out when I wasn't buying anything.

My primary concern while writing (or more accurately, compiling) this book was establishing the veracity of the quotes used in it. Simply, were the statements actually said? There are some great oft-repeated quotes "out there" that I didn't use, simply because I wasn't satisfied that the statements actually took place. After researching, I'm convinced Lord Kelvin didn't say all the stupid things that are routinely attributed to him, nor that Elvis Presley was told by someone at the Grand Old Opry to go back to his day job. The famous quote of IBM head Thomas Watson's prediction of a market of five computers doesn't hold up under scrutiny. And on and on...

The Internet, while a remarkable collective resource (and indispensable to the making of this book), is a crap shoot as far as research goes. It is, by nature, an undisciplined medium. The quality of sites varies dramatically from very credible to not credible whatsoever, and thus requires a considerable amount of scrutiny. Several sites exist dedicated specifically to quotes, but how accurate are they? In the end, I used some of these sites as a starting point for research, but I didn't use them as sources.

Which brings us to a second issue: what exactly constitutes an accurate quote? Consider this —

1 Samuel 17:44 from the *King James Bible* —

> "And the Philistine said to David, Come to me, and I will give thy flesh unto the fowls of the air, and to the beasts of the field."

The same passage in the *Holman Christian Standard Bible* —

> "Come here," the Philistine called to David, "and I'll give your flesh to the birds of the sky and the wild beasts!"

And in the *New Living Translation* —

> "Come over here, and I'll give your flesh to the birds and wild animals!" Goliath yelled.

Aside from the event preceding the English language of King James by 2,500 years, all these translations are different. So, which one is correct?

Well, none of them, if the standard is verbatim. But all of them are, if the standard is staying as close as possible to the original wording with an intention to accurately convey the meaning within the context of when the statement was made. I think any reasonable person would read the three quotes above and conclude they all amount to the same thing.

A more modern example is Dick Rowe's statement when he and Decca Records turned down the Beatles. The quote is taken from Hunter Davies' *The Beatles: The Authorized Biography,* and the words come directly from Beatles manager Brian Epstein. Referring to Rowe, Epstein said, "He told me they didn't like the sound. Groups of guitars were on the way out." The comment was made in March 1962 and the quote was first printed in 1968, with Epstein making the statement sometime in the interim. But did he remember it exactly as it happened?

Assuming he did, the most accurate way to use the quote is exactly as Epstein said it: "He told me they didn't like the sound. Groups of guitars were on the way out." But the quote is a little more pungent when, instead of Epstein's re-telling, one actually has Dick Rowe saying, "We don't like the sound. Groups of guitars are on the way out." But is it okay to do that?

Along the same line, we have the quote regarding Thomas Edison —

The source is *Edison Inventing the Century* by Neil Baldwin. But the actual quote is from Thomas Edison himself, many years after the event had taken place. Edison said, "One day I heard the teacher tell the visiting school inspector that I was addled and it would not be worthwhile keeping me in school any longer." Aside from the change in third-person to first-person, did Edison paraphrase? Did he leave something out? Did he summarize a long conversation into one compound sentence? Does it matter?

My judgment is that it doesn't. It seems clear to me, regardless of the exact way these quotes were stated, Goliath didn't think much of David, Edison's teacher had a low opinion of Edison, and Dick Rowe didn't hold the Beatles in very high regard. There is no way we can know how each of these was exactly stated, but the essence of what each conveys is very clear. If these quotes are not exact, they are very, very close.

Further, all these quotes succinctly sum up their respective opinions within the context that the quotes took place. Context is not just important – its inclusion is a paramount and integral part of any accurate restatement, or any presentation, really. Words and statements divorced from their time, place, and circumstance can become misleading, distorted, and sometimes even dangerous, assuming a life of their own which was never intended. One often sees such gross caricatures in political sound bites. Aside from the primary importance of just getting it right, the context sets up the other half of this book: the story behind the quote.

And so, the standards I used when compiling this book:

1. A quote had to be verifiable from what I judged a legitimate source.
2. When the exact wording of a quote was clearly at hand, it was used.
3. If the quote originated from a re-telling or a situation in which the exact wording was not available, the quote was presented in the book in a matter that was as close as possible to the re-telling with no embellishment, with changes limited to tense and pronoun changes reflecting first, second and third persons.
4. The context of the quote was presented as accurately as possible.

G. R. Howard

Sources Cited

p. 2 "1 Samuel 17:44." *King James Bible (Authorized Version).* King James Bible Online, 2015. Web. 22 Feb 2015.

p. 4 Baldwin, Neil. *Edison: Inventing the Century.* New York: Hyperion, 1995. Print., pp. 24–25.

p. 6 Avid, Hazel B. and Catherine Ruddiman. *Henry Ford: Young Man with Ideas.* New York: Simon & Schuster, 1986. Print., p. 159.

p. 8 Wyatt, Robert and John Andrew Johnson, ed. *The George Gershwin Reader.* New York: Oxford University Press, 2004. Print., p. 31.

p. 10 Kelley, Kitty. *Oprah.* New York: Crown Publishers, 2010. Print., p. 109.

p. 12 Weintraub, Robert. *The House That Ruth Built: A New Stadium, the First Yankees Championship, and the Redemption of 1923.* Boston: Little, Brown and Company, 2011. Print., p. 38.

p. 14 Isaacson, Walter. *Einstein: His Life and Universe.* New York: Simon & Schuster, 2007. Print., pp. 34–35.

p. 16 Panabaker, James. *Shelby Foote and the Art of History: Two Gates to the City.* Knoxville: University of Tennessee Press, 2004. Print., p. 159.

p. 18 Sandburg, Carl. *Abraham Lincoln: The Prairie Years and the War Years.* New York: Sterling Publishing, 2007. Print., p. 213.

p. 20 Rebello, Kathy with Amy Cortese and Rob Hof. "Inside Microsoft." *Business Week.* Bloomberg L.P., 15 July 1996. Web. 2 Nov 2014.

p. 22 McCullough, David. *1776.* New York: Simon & Schuster, 2005. Print., p. 265.

p. 24 Bascomb, Neil. *The Perfect Mile: Three Athletes, One Goal, and Less Than Four Minutes to Achieve It.* New York: Houghton Mifflin Harcourt, 2004. Print., p. 57.

p. 26 Cawthorne, Nigel. *Amazing Guitar Facts and Trivia.* New York: Chartwell Books, Inc., 2011. Print., p. 45.

p. 28 Coffey, Wayne. *The Boys of Winter: The Untold Story of a Coach, a Dream, and the 1980 U.S. Olympic Hockey Team.* New York: Three Rivers Press, 2005. Print., p. 26.

p. 30 Chisholm, Archibald J. *The First Kuwait Oil Concession Agreement: A Record of the Negotiations, 1911–1934.* New York: Frank Cass & Company, 1975. Print., p 109.

p. 32 Theoharis, Jeanne. *The Rebellious Life of Mrs. Rosa Parks.* Boston: Beacon Press, 2013. Print., p. 62.

p. 34 Isaacson, Walter. *Steve Jobs.* New York: Simon & Schuster Paperbacks, 2011. Print., p. 137.

p. 36 Yarow, Jay. "Here's What Steve Ballmer Thought About the iPhone Five Years Ago." *Business Insider.* Business Insider Inc., 29 Jun 2012. Web. 25 Jan 2015.

p. 38 Roper, Elmo. "It's Dewey Over Truman by a Landslide." *The Evening Independent [St. Augustine]* 9 Sep 1948, 41st ed., sec. 266: 1–2. *Google News.* Google. Web. 7 Oct 2014.

p. 40 Spalding, Francis. *Roger Fry: Art and Life.* Oakland, CA: University of California Press, 1980. Print., p. 136.

p. 42 Blotner, Joseph Leo. *Faulkner: A Biography.* Jackson, MS: University of Mississippi Press, 1974. Print., pp. 117–118.

p. 44 Anderson, Christopher. *Barbra: The Way She Is.* New York: William Morrow, 2006. Print., p. 38.

p. 46 Bigold, Pat. "The Flop That Flabbergasted." *Star Advertiser.* Honolulu Star-Bulletin, 13 Feb 1999. Web. 7 July 2014.

p. 48 Martin, George. *All You Need Is Ears: The Inside Personal Story of the Genius Who Created the Beatles.* New York: St.Martin's Press, 1979. Print., p. 159.

p. 50 O'Toole, Garson. "Beatles Rejection: We Don't Like Their Sound. Groups of Guitars Are on Their Way Out." *Quote Investigator.* Garson O'Toole, 27 Apr 2013. Web. 17 Oct 2014.

p. 52 Norman, Phillip. *Shout!: The Beatles in Their Generation.* New York: Simon & Schuster, 1981. Print., p. 35.

p. 54 Koszarski, Richard. *Hollywood on the Hudson: Film and Television in New York from Griffith to Sarnoff.* Piscataway, NJ: Rutgers University Press, 2008. Print., p. 149.

p. 56 Scarfone, Jay and William Skillman. *The Wizard of Oz: The Official 75th Anniversary Companion.* New York: Harper's Design, 2013. Print., p. 157.

p. 58 Stump, Al. *Cobb.* Chapel Hill, NC: Algonquin Books, 1994. Print., p. 44.

p. 60 Jordan, David. *Pete Rose: A Biography.* Westport, CT: Greenwood Press, 2004. Print., p. 12.

p. 62 PennLive Editorial Board. "Retraction for Our 1863 Editorial Calling Gettysburg Address 'Silly Remarks': Editorial." *Penn Live: The Patriot-News.* PA Media Group, 24 Nov 2013. Web. 20 Jan 2014.

p. 64 Hauser, Thomas. *Muhammad Ali: His Life and Times.* New York: Simon & Schuster, 1991. Print., p. 68.

p. 66 "De Forest Says Space Travel Is Impossible." *Lewiston Morning Tribune,* 25 Feb 1957: 7. *Google News.* Google. Web. 11 Nov 2014.

p. 68 Flink, Steve. "Steve Flink: Flink on Kramer." *Tennis Channel.* The Tennis Channel, 18 Dec 2007. Web. 23 Nov 2014.

p. 70 Henshaw, Peter. *Mustang.* New York: Chartwell Books, 2013. Print., p. 38.

p. 72 Newcomb, Simon. "Is the Airship Coming?" *McClure's Magazine,* 17 Sep 1901: 435. Mississippi State University Library. Web. 21 Feb 2015.

p. 74 Kauffman, Stanford B. *Pan Am Pioneer: A Manager's Memoir from Seaplane Clippers to Jumbo Jets.* Lubbock: Texas Tech University Press, 1995. Print., p. 192.

p. 76 "Citizen Kane." *Movie-Film-Review.* Chris Tookey, 2002–2009. Web. 29 Sep 2014.

p. 78 Zimaneck, Brad. "Revenge Is Sweet: Favre Dismantles Team That Traded Him." *JSOnline.com.* Journal Sentinel Inc., 1995. Web. 2 Dec 2014.

p. 80 "Peyton Manning Likely Will Never Play Football Again, Sources Say." *Los Angeles Times.* Los Angeles Times, 31 Jan 2012. Web. 11 July 2014.

p. 82 Sacks, Ethan. "Spider-Man Got His Start as a Fly on the Wall of Marvel's Stan Lee." *NYDailyNews.com.* NYDailyNews.com, 27 June 2012. Web. 30 Sep 2014.

p. 84 "Ted Turner & CNN." *The Pop History Dig.* The Pop History Dig, LLC, 29 Nov 2008. Last updated 30 Aug 2014. Web. 22 Oct 2014.

Whittemore, Hank. *CNN: The Inside Story.* Boston: Little, Brown and Company, 1980. Print., p. 31.

p. 86 Beaumont, Daniel. *Preachin' the Blues: The Life and Times of Son House.* New York: Oxford University Press, 2011. Print., p. 89.

p. 88 Layden, Joe. *The Last Great Fight.* New York: St. Martin's Press, 2007. Print., p. 2.

p. 90 Ash, Mary Kay. *Miracles Happen: The Life and Timeless Principles of the Founder of Mary Kay Inc.* New York: HarperCollins Publishers Inc., 1981. Print., p. 4, p. 9.

p. 92 Hillenbrand, Laura. *Seabiscuit: An American Legend.* New York: Ballantine Books, 2001. Print., p. 38.

p. 94 "Imagining The Internet: A History and Forecast." *Elon University.* Elon University School of Communications, n.d. Web. 25 Oct 2014.

p. 96 "Wilma (Glodean) Rudolph (1940–1994)." *Bio.* A&E Television Networks, 2015. Web. 31 Jan 2015.

p. 98 Gilbert, Martin. *Churchill: A Life.* New York: Henry Holt and Company, 1991. Print., p. 38.

p. 100 Wahlberg, Bjorn. "United Artists Rejection Letter." *Starwarz.com.* Starkiller, 4 Mar 2010. Web. 8 Nov 2014.

p. 102 White, Dana. *George Lucas.* Minneapolis: Lerner Publications Company, 2000. Print., p. 19.

p. 104 Haddix, Chuck. *Bird: The Life and Music of Charlie Parker.* Urbana: University of Illinois Press, 2013. Print., pp. 15–16.

p. 106 Devito, Carlo. *Yogi Berra: The Life and Times of an American Original.* Chicago: Triumph Books, 2008. Print., p. 32.

p. 108 Mendelsohn, John. "Led Zeppelin I." *Rolling Stone.* Rolling Stone, 15 March 1969. Web. 15 Oct 2014.

p. 110 Fischer, David Hackett. *Washington's Crossing.* New York: Oxford University Press, 2004. Print., p. 205.

p. 112 "Snow White and the Seven Dwarves." *Movie-Film-Review.* Chris Tookey, 2009–2014. Web. 8 July 2014.

p. 114 "The Rolling Stones Still Rocking 50 Years After 1st Gig." *City News Toronto.* Rogers Media, 12 July 2012. Web. 15 Oct 2014.

p. 116 Osteen, Joel. *Become a Better You.* New York: Howard Books, 2008. Print., p. 138.

p. 118 Leavy, Jane. *Sandy Koufax: A Lefty's Legacy.* New York: HarperCollins Publishers, 2002. Print., p. 64, p. 93.

p. 120 Scaduto, Anthony. "Bob Dylan: An Intimate Biography, Part One." *Rolling Stone.* Rolling Stone, 2 Mar 1972. Web. 30 Nov 2014.

p. 122 Cash, Johnny. *The Autobiography of Johnny Cash.* New York: HarperCollins Publishers, 1997. Print., p. 181.

p. 124 Guralnick, Peter. *Last Train to Memphis: The Rise of Elvis Presley.* New York: Little, Brown and Company, 1994. Print., p. 83, p. 93.

p. 126 Freeman, Michael. *ESPN: The Uncensored History.* Lanham, MD: Rowman & Littlefield, 2001. Print., p. 103.

p. 128 Lewis, Roger. *The Life and Death of Peter Sellers.* New York: Applause Books, 1997. Print., p. 308.

p. 130 Felton, Bruce. *What Were They Thinking? Really Bad Ideas Throughout History.* Guilford, CT: Lyons Press, 2007. Print., p. 80.

p. 132 "John Coltrane and Eric Dolphy Answer the Jazz Critics." *Downbeat.* Maher Publications, 12 Apr 1962. Web. 30 Nov 2014.

p. 134 Lapsley, Phil. "The Greatest 'Bad Business Decision' Quotation That Never Was." *The History of Phone Phreaking Blog.* Phil Lapsley, 8 Jan 2011. Web. 3 Nov 2014.

p. 136 Badame, Emma. "30 Days of Bond: The Sean Connery Years." *Cineplex.* Cineplex Entertainment LP, 9 Oct 2012. Web. 19 Jan 2015.

p. 138 Orfalea, Paul and Ann Marsh. *Copy This: Lessons from a Hyperactive Dyslexic Who Turned a Bright Idea into a Company Called Kinko's.* New York: Workman Publishing, Inc., 2007. Print., p. xxi, p. 5.

p. 140 "Margaret Thatcher: A Life in Words." *The Telegraph.* Telegraph Media Group Limited, 4 Apr 2013. Web. 1 Feb 2015.

p. 142 Nack, William. *Secretariat: The Making of a Champion.* New York: Da Capo Press Books, 2002. Print., p. 84, p. 303.

p. 144 "Grand Canyon." *Grand Canyon National Park.* Grandcanyon-nationalpark.org, 2013. Web. 14 Oct 2014.

p. 146 Ridley, Mark. *The Cooperative Gene: How Mendel's Demon Explains the Evolution of Complex Beings.* New York: The Free Press, 2001. Print., p. 3.

p. 148 "You Ain't Seen Nothin' Yet." *Variety.* Variety Media, LLC, 16 Oct 2005. Web. 4 Nov 2014.

p. 150 Belsham, William. *Memoirs of the Reign of George III to the Session of Parliament Ending A.D. 1793, Volume II.* London, G.G. and J. Robinson, 1801. Print., p. 58.

p. 152 Robinson, David. *Chaplin, the Mirror of Opinion.* Bloomington: Indiana University Press, 1983. Print., p. 20.

p. 154 Chaplin, Charlie. *My Autobiography.* Brooklyn: Melville House, 1964. Print., p. 159.

p. 156 "Did Tris Speaker Predict That the Yankees Made a Mistake Turning Babe Ruth into an Outfielder?" *Sports Urban Legends Revealed.* Sports Urban Legends Revealed!. Web. 1 Feb 2015.

p. 158 Walker, Audrey. *Audrey: Her Real Story.* New York: St. Martin's Press, 1994. Print., p. 42.

p. 160 Henshaw, Peter. *The Ultimate Encyclopedia of the Corvette.* New York: Chartwell Books, 2004. Print., p. 23.

p. 162 Branscomb, Lewis M. and Philip E. Auerswald. *Taking Technical Risks: How Innovators, Executives, and Investors Manage High-Tech Risks.* Cambridge: MIT Press, 2001. Print., p. 63.

p. 164 "The Unlikely Casting of Dustin Hoffman in *The Graduate.*" *AMC.* AMC Network Entertainment LLC, Apr 2008. Web. 1 Feb 2015.

p. 166 Gruver, Ed. *The American Football League: A Year-By-Year History,* 1960–1969. Jefferson, N.C.: McFarland & Company, Inc., 1997. Print., p. 217.

p. 168 Morton, David. "Exploring The History of the Recording Business." *Recording History.* David Morton, 1998–2006. Web. 20 Feb 2015.

p. 170 Hamilton, Tyler J. *Mad Like Tesla: Underdog Inventors and Their Relentless Pursuit of Clean Energy.* Toronto: ECW Press, 2011. Print., p. 11.

p. 172 Mathison, Keith. "Luther, Calvin, and Copernicus — A Reformed Approach to Science and Scripture." *Ligonier.org.* Ligonier Ministries, 1 Jun 2012. Web. 17 Oct 2014.

p. 174 Blackmore, David S.T. *Warfare on the Mediterranean in the Age of Sail: A History 1571–1866.* Jefferson, NC: McFarland, 2011. Print., p. 295.

p. 176 Carey, Bjorn. "You're Right, Rockets Do Work in Space." *Popular Science.* Popular Science, 20 Jul 2009. Web. 17 Oct 2014.

p. 178 O'Toole, Garson. "Can't Act; Slightly Bald; Can Dance a Little." *Quote Investigator.* Garson O'Toole, 7 Aug 2014. Web. 17 Oct 2014.

p. 180 "Gone with the Wind Study Guide." *Film Education.* Film Education, 1995. Web. 14 Oct 2014.

p. 182 Low, Chris. "Harper Emerges from Backup Role to Become History-making QB." *ESPN.* ESPN Internet Ventures, 12 Nov 2007. Web. 5 Oct 2014.

p. 184 Shapiro, Susan. "Regrets, Even Critics Have a Few." *The Wall Street Journal.* Dow Jones & Company, Inc., 11 Sep 2012. Web. 17 Oct 2014.

p. 186 Bowker, Gordon. *James Joyce.* New York: Farrar, Straus and Giroux, 2011. Print., p. 307.

p. 188 "Pauline Kael Reviews A–Z." *Geocities.com.* n.p., n.d. Web. 2 Feb 2015.

p. 190 Abt, Samuel. *Lemond: The Incredible Comeback of an American Hero.* New York: Random House, 1990. Print., p. 186.

p. 192 Manso, Peter. *Brando: The Biography.* New York: Hyperion, 1994. Print., pp. 103–4.

p. 194 Biskind, Peter. *Easy Riders, Raging Bulls: How the Sex, Drugs, and Rock 'n' Roll Generation Saved Hollywood.* New York: Touchstone, 1999. Print., p. 154.

p. 196 Heylin, Clinton, ed. *All Yesterday's Parties: The Velvet Underground in Print, 1966–1971.* New York: Da Capo Press, 2005. Print., p. 52.

p. 198 Rewald, John. *Georges Seurat.* New York: Wittenberk & Company, 1946. Print., p. 317.

p. 200 Pepys, Samuel. "Monday 29 September 1662." *The Diary of Samuel Pepys M.A. F.R.S. Covent Garden: George Bell & Sons, 1893.* N. p., *The Diary of Samuel Pepys: Daily Entries from the 17th Century London Diary*. Pepysdiary.com, Jan 2003. Web. 21 Feb 2015.

p. 202 "Voltaire, Shakespeare, and Canada." *Canadian Adaptations of Shakespeare Project.* Daniel Fischlin, 2004. Web. 28 Sep 2014.

p. 204 Lockwood, Lewis. *Beethoven: The Music & the Life.* New York: W.W. Norton & Company, Inc., 2003. Print., p. 439.

Bibliography

"1 Mile Run World Record Progression." *Berkshire Sports.* n.p., n.d. Web. 7 Oct 2014.

"1 Samuel 17:44." *King James Bible (Authorized Version).* King James Bible Online, 2015. Web. 22 Feb 2015.

"100 Best Novels." *Modern Library.* Random House LLC, 1995–2014. Web. 13 Oct 2014.

"100 Greatest Debut Albums." *Uncut* Aug 2006: 48–71. Print.

"100 Years of Einstein: Miraculous Visions." *The Economist.* The Economist Newspaper Limited, 29 Dec 2004. Web. 6 Oct 2014.

"100 Years...100 Songs." *American Film Institute.* American Film Institute, 2004–2015. Web. 11 Jan 2015.

"500 Greatest Albums of All Time." *Rolling Stone.* Rolling Stone, 31 May 2012. Web. 19 Oct 2014.

"A Biography of Lord North (1713–1792)." *American History from Revolution to Reconstruction and Beyond.* George M. Welling and the University of Groningen, 1994–2012. Web. 23 Oct 2014.

"A Capsule History of the Bell System." *Beatriceco.com.* Beatrice Companies, Inc., 1994–2014. Web. 28 Sep 2014.

"A380." *Airbus.com.* Airbus SAS, 2014. Web. 13 Nov 2014.

"About Joel Osteen." *Joel Osteen Ministries.* Joel Osteen Ministries, 2014. Web. 19 Jul 2014.

"About Johnny Cash." *CMT.com.* Viacom International Inc., 2014. Web. 28 Sep 2014.

"About Paul Orfalea." *Orfalea College of Business.* California Polytechnic State University, 2012. Web. 11 Mar 2015.

Abt, Samuel. *Lemond: The Incredible Comeback of an American Hero.* New York: Random House, 1990. Print.

Acocella, Nick. "Berra Was Great, Which Was as Close to Good as Possible." *ESPN*. ESPN Internet Ventures, updated 18 Oct 2006. Web. 30 Sep 2014.

"AFI's 100 Years...100 Movies — 10th Anniversary Edition." *American Film Institute*. American Film Institute, 2015. Web. 26 Jan 2015.

"AFI's 100 Years...100 Movies." *American Film Institute*. American Film Institute, 2015. Web. 26 Jan 2015.

Ahonen, Tomi. "Digital Divide: Global Household Penetration Rates for Technology." *VR*. VR World Media Hong Kong Ltd, 26 Jan 2011. Web. 22 Feb 2015.

"American President: Ulysses S. Grant (1822–1885)." *Miller Center*. Rector and Visitors of the University of Virginia, 2014. Web. 16 Oct 2014.

"America's Greatest Legends." *American Film Institute*. American Film Institute, 2014. Web. 23 Oct 2014.

"An Inventor with a Business Head: Edison Tells How He Made Phonographs Pay, While the Company Didn't." *The New York Times*. The New York Times Company, 13 Sep 1894. Web. 29 Sep 2014.

Anderson, Christopher. *Barbra: The Way She Is*. New York: William Morrow, 2006. Print.

Ash, Mary Kay. *Miracles Happen: The Life and Timeless Principles of the Founder of Mary Kay Inc.* New York: HarperCollins Publishers Inc., 1981. Print.

Avid, Hazel B. and Catherine Ruddiman. *Henry Ford: Young Man with Ideas*. New York: Simon & Schuster, 1986. Print.

"Award Ceremony Speech." *Nobelprize.org*. Nobel Media AB, 2014. Web. 19 Feb 2015.

Bacon, Tony. *50 Years of Fender*. London: Balaton Books, 2000. Print.

Badame, Emma. "30 Days of Bond: The Sean Connery Years." *Cineplex*. Cineplex Entertainment LP, 9 Oct 2012. Web. 19 Jan 2015.

Badenhouse, Kurt. "Apple Dominates List of World's Most Valuable Brands." *Forbes.com*. Forbes.com LLC, 6 Nov 2013. Web. 20 Jan 2014.

Baldwin, Neil. *Edison: Inventing the Century.* New York: Hyperion, 1995. Print.

"Barbra Streisand: Biography." *IMDb.* IMDb.com, Inc., 1990–2014. Web. 17 Nov 2014.

Barrier, Michael. *Hollywood Cartoons: American Animation in Its Golden Age.* New York: Oxford University Press, 1999. Print.

Bascomb, Neil. *The Perfect Mile: Three Athletes, One Goal, and Less than Four Minutes to Achieve It.* New York: Houghton Mifflin Harcourt, 2004. Print.

Beardsley, Roger and Daniel Leech-Wilkinson. "A Brief History of Recording to Ca. 1950." *CHARM.* King's College London, 2009. Web. 28 Sep 2014.

"Beatles Albums Offered on iTunes." *BBC News.* BBC, 16 Nov 2010. Web. 19 Oct 2014.

Beaumont, Daniel. *Preachin' the Blues: The Life and Times of Son House.* New York: Oxford University Press, 2011. Print.

Bellfield, Lee. "This Month in Boxing History: Buster Douglas–Mike Tyson 1990." *SaddoBoxing.com.* Saddo Boxing, 16 Feb 2006. Web. 29 Sep 2014.

Belsham, William. *Memoirs of the Reign of George III to the Session of Parliament Ending A.D. 1793, Volume II.* London, G.G. and J. Robinson, 1801. Print.

Benaroya, Adam. "The Jewish Roots in George Gershwin's Music." *I. L. Peretz Community Jewish School.* I. L. Peretz Community Jewish School, May 2000. Web. 8 Jul 2014.

Benzinga Editorial. "Apple Now Most Valuable Company in History." *Forbes.com.* Forbes.com LLC, 21 Aug 2012. Web. 8 Jul 2014.

Bigold, Pat. "The Flop That Flabbergasted." *Star Advertiser.* Honolulu Star-Bulletin, 13 Feb 1999. Web. 7 Jul 2014.

"Bio." *The Official Website of Brett Favre.* OfficialBrettFavre.com, 2015. Web. 1 March 2015.

Biskind, Peter. *Easy Riders, Raging Bulls: How the Sex, Drugs, and Rock 'n' Roll Generation Saved Hollywood.* New York: Touchstone, 1999. Print.

Blackmore, David S.T. *Warfare on the Mediterranean in the Age of Sail: A History 1571–1866.* Jefferson, NC: McFarland, 2011. Print.

Blodget, Henry. "Apple's iPhone Business Alone Is Now Bigger than All of Microsoft." *Business Insider.* Business Insider Inc., 12 Feb 2012. Web. 7 Jul 2014.

Blotner, Joseph Leo. *Faulkner: A Biography.* Jackson, MS: University of Mississippi Press, 1974. Print.

Bond, Paul. "Study: Global Entertainment Industry Poised to Top $2 Trillion in 2016." *The Hollywood Reporter.* The Hollywood Reporter, 5 Jun 2013. Web. 6 Nov 2014.

Bort, Julie. "Steve Wozniak Thought the First Macintosh Was a 'Lousy Computer' That 'Failed.' " *Business Insider.* Business Insider Inc., 27 Jun 2013. Web. 20 Jan 2014.

Bowker, Gordon. *James Joyce.* New York: Farrar, Straus and Giroux, 2011. Print.

Branscomb, Lewis M. and Philip E. Auerswald. *Taking Technical Risks: How Innovators, Executives, and Investors Manage High-Tech Risks.* Cambridge: MIT Press, 2001. Print.

"Brett Favre." *Databasefootball.com.* DatabaseSports.com, 2002–2011. Web. 17 Nov 2014.

Brown, Ivor. "Agate, James Evershed (1877–1947)." *Oxford Dictionary of National Biography.* Oxford University Press, 2004; online edn, Jan 2011. Web. 3 Oct 2014.

Brown, Raymond. *The James Bond Bedside Companion.* New York: Galahad Books, 1984. Print.

Brozyna, Andrew. *Books for Victory.* Andrew Brozyna, 18 May 2013. Web. 2 Feb 2015

Buncombe, Andrew. "The Grandfather of Rock'n'roll: The Devil's Instrument." *The Independent.* Independent.co.uk, 26 Jul 2006. Web. 29 Sep 2014.

Burnton, Simon. "50 Stunning Olympic Moments No. 28: Dick Fosbury Introduces 'The Flop.' " *The Guardian.* Guardian News and Media Limited, 8 May 2012. Web. 19 Nov 2014.

Carey, Bjorn. "You're Right, Rockets Do Work in Space." *Popular Science.* Popular Science, 20 Jul 2009. Web. 17 Oct 2014.

"Carlo Ponti, Film Producer, Dies at 94." *The New York Times.* The New York Times Company, 11 Jan 2007. Web. 28 Sep 2014.

"Carlo Ponti." *The Independent.* Independent.co.uk, 11 Jan 2007. Web. 28 Sep 2014.

Cash, Johnny. *The Autobiography of Johnny Cash.* New York: HarperCollins Publishers, 1997. Print.

Cawthorne, Nigel. *Amazing Guitar Facts and Trivia.* New York: Chartwell Books, Inc., 2011. Print.

"CBS News Poll: Who Was the Best James Bond?" *CBS News.* CBS Interactive, Inc., 10 Aug 2014. Web. 14 Dec 2014.

Chaplin, Charlie. *My Autobiography.* Brooklyn: Melville House, 1964. Print.

"Charles Bluhdorn: The Mad Austrian." *Jackfsanders.tripod.com.* n.p., n.d. Web. 28 Sep 2014.

Chawla, Jatin. "Copy Machine Supply — A Brief History of Xerox." *Articlesbase.* ArticlesBase.com, 24 Jul 2006, updated 25 Aug 2009. Web. 1 Feb 2015.

"Chester F. Carlson." *The Great Idea Finder.* The Great Idea Finder, revised 21 Jun 2006. Web. 26 Oct 2014.

"Chevrolet Corvette History." *Edmunds.com.* Edmunds.com, Inc., n.d. Web. 9 Nov 2014.

Chisholm, Archibald J. *The First Kuwait Oil Concession Agreement: A Record of the Negotiations, 1911–1934.* New York: Frank Cass & Company, 1975. Print

"Citizen Kane." *Movie-Film-Review.* Chris Tookey, 2002–2009. Web. 29 Sep 2014.

Cocks, Jay. "When the Music Died." *Time* 22 Dec 1980: 116–25. Print.

Coffey, Wayne. *The Boys of Winter: The Untold Story of a Coach, a Dream, and the 1980 U.S. Olympic Hockey Team.* New York: Three Rivers Press, 2005. Print.

Cole, Richard with Richard Turbo. *Stairway to Heaven: Led Zeppelin Uncensored.* New York: HarperCollins Publishers, 2002. Print.

Collins, Bud. "Bjorn Borg." *ATP World Tour.* ATP Tour, Inc., 1994–2014. Web. 23 Nov 2014.

Cooke, Alistair. *Letter from America, 1946–2004.* New York: Knopf Doubleday Publishing Group, 2007. Print.

Corrigan, Maureen. "How 'Gatsby' Went from a Moldering Flop to a Great American Novel." *NPR.* NPR Services, 8 Sep 2014. Web. 5 Oct 2014.

Corrigan, Maureen. "Why 'The Great Gatsby' Is the 'Greatest' of All." Interview. *USA Today.* USA Today, 10 Sep 2014. Web. 30 Sept 2014.

Cotter, Holland. "Art Review; How Seurat Worked Up to Sunday." *The New York Times.* The New York Times Company, 20 Aug 2004. Web. 13 Oct 2014.

Cruh, George and Walter Carter. *Electric Guitars and Basses.* New York: Backbeat Books, 2010. Print.

"De Forest Says Space Travel Is Impossible." *Lewiston Morning Tribune,* 25 Feb 1957: 7. *Google News.* Google. Web. 11 Nov 2014.

DeMichael, Tom. *James Bond FAQ.* Milwaukee: Applause Theatre & Cinema Books, 2013. Print.

Devito, Carlo. *Yogi Berra: The Life and Times of an American Original.* Chicago: Triumph Books, 2008. Print.

"Did Tris Speaker Predict That the Yankees Made a Mistake Turning Babe Ruth into an Outfielder?" *Sports Urban Legends Revealed.* Sports Urban Legends Revealed!, 1 Feb 2015.

Dirks, Tim. "The History of Film: The 1970s." *AMC Filmsite.* American Movie Classics Company LLC, 2014. Web. 8 Nov 2014.

Dunaway, James. "Track and Field; From Impossible to Commonplace." *The New York Times.* The New York Times Company, 4 May 2003. Web. 19 Feb 2015.

Durso, James. "Fearless Fosbury Flops to Glory." *New York Times: This Day in Sports.* The New York Times Company, 20 Oct 1968. Web. 8 July 2014.

"Dustin Hoffman: Awards." *IMDb.* IMDb.com, Inc., 1990–2014. Web. 14 Oct 2014.

"E-Commerce in Real Time." *Ever Merchant.* Ever Merchant, LLC, 2014. Web. 22 Mar 2015.

Ellis, Aaron. "Track and Field: What Is the Straddle Technique in High Jump?" *Quora.* Quora, Inc. 6 June 2012. Web. 23 Nov 2014.

" 'Elvis 75' Hundred-Song Box Set Celebrates Late Rock Singer's 75th Birthday." *The Independent.* Independent.co.uk, 19 Oct 2009. Web. 4 Nov 2014.

"Elvis Presley: Biography." *Rolling Stone.* Rolling Stone, 2014. Web. 4 Nov 2014.

Erb, Jane. "George Gershwin." *Classical Net.* Jane Erb, 1996. Web. 17 Nov 2014.

"ESPN International Fact Sheet." *ESPNMediazone.com.* ESPN MediaZone, 2014. Web. 14 Dec 2014.

Ewen, David. A Journey to Greatness: *The Life & Music of George Gershwin.* New York: Holy & Co., 1956. Print.

Felton, Bruce. *What Were They Thinking? Really Bad Ideas Throughout History.* Guilford, CT: Lyons Press, 2007. Print.

Ferrell, Robert H. *Harry S Truman: A Life.* Columbia, MO: University of Missouri Press, 1994. Print.

Fischer, David Hackett. *Washington's Crossing.* New York: Oxford University Press, 2004. Print.

Flink, Steve. "Steve Flink: Flink on Kramer." *Tennis Channel.* The Tennis Channel, 18 Dec 2007. Web. 23 Nov 2014.

"Ford Mustang History." *Edmunds.com.* Edmunds.com, Inc., 2014. Web. 19 Nov 2014.

"Fred Astaire." *Reel Classics.* Reel Classics, LLC, 19 Oct 2010. Web. 23 Oct 2014.

Freeman, Michael. *ESPN: The Uncensored History.* Lanham, MD: Rowman & Littlefield, 2001. Print.

Funck, Larry. "Pasteur vs. Pouchet and the Demise of Spontaneous Generation: Lessons for Today from an Old Controversy, Part 1." *The BioLogos Forum.* The BioLogos Foundation, 31 Mar 2014. Web. 1 Feb 2015.

Gabler, Neal. *Walt Disney: The Triumph of the American Imagination.* New York: Vintage Books, 2006. Print.

Garner, Leslie. "Leslie Garner Meets the Legendary Actress as She Prepares for This Week's Unicef Gala Performance." *The Sunday Telegraph,* 26 May 1991. *Audrey Hepburn: A Tribute To Her Humanitarian Work.* Sally & Clara, 2001. Web. 28 Sep 2014.

Gash, Norman. "Jenkinson, Robert Banks, Second Earl of Liverpool (1770–1828)." *Oxford Dictionary of National Biography.* Oxford University Press, 2004; online edn, Jan 2008. Web. 5 Oct 2014.

George-Warren, Leslie, and Patricia Romanowski, ed. *The Rolling Stone Encyclopedia of The Rock & Roll.* New York: Fireside Press, 2001. Print.

Gilbert, Martin. *Churchill: A Life.* New York: Henry Holt and Company, 1991. Print.

Gilmore, Mikal. *Stories Done: Writings on the 1960s and Its Discontents.* New York: Free Press, 2008. Print.

Gomery, Douglas. "Writing the History of the American Film Industry: Warner Brothers and Sound." Nichols, Bill, ed. *Movies and Methods: An Anthology, Volume 2.* Berkeley: The University of California Press, 1985. Print.

"Gone with the Wind (1939) Trivia." *IMDb.* IMDb.com, Inc., 1990–2015. Web. 1 Feb 2015.

"Gone with the Wind Study Guide." *Film Education.* Film Education, 1995. Web. 14 Oct 2014.

"Grand Canyon." *Grand Canyon National Park.* Grandcanyon-nationalpark.org, 2013. Web. 14 Oct 2014.

"Grand Canyon." *National Park Service.* Department of the Interior, 2014. Web. 3 Oct 2014.

"Great Britons." *BBC.co.uk.* BBC, 14 May 2006. Web. 30 Sep 2014.

Griffin, Farah Jasmin and Salim Washington. *Clawing at the Limits of Cool: Miles Davis, John Coltrane, and the Greatest Jazz Collaboration Ever.* New York: Thomas Dunne, 2008. Print.

Gross, Daniel, et al. "Betting the Company: Joseph Wilson and the Xerox 914." *Forbes Greatest Business Stories of All Time.* New York: John Wiley & Sons, 1996. n. pag. *Stephen Hicks, Ph.D.* Stephen Hicks, Jan 2012. Web. 22 Feb 2015.

Grutz, Jane Waldron. "Prelude to Discovery." *Saudi Aramco World,* Jan/Feb 1999: 30–35. Aramco Services Company, 2004–2014. Web. 11 Nov 2014.

Gruver, Ed. *The American Football League: A Year-By-Year History, 1960–1969.* Jefferson, N.C.: McFarland & Company, Inc., 1997. Print.

Guralnick, Peter. *Last Train to Memphis: The Rise of Elvis Presley.* New York: Little, Brown and Company, 1994. Print.

Haddix, Chuck. *Bird: The Life and Music of Charlie Parker.* Urbana: University of Illinois Press, 2013. Print.

Halsall, Paul. "The Crime of Galileo: Indictment and Abjuration of 1633." *Modern History Sourcebook.* Paul Halsall, Jul 1998, rev. Jan 1999. Web. 17 Oct 2014.

Hamilton, Tyler J. *Mad Like Tesla: Underdog Inventors and Their Relentless Pursuit of Clean Energy.* Toronto: ECW Press, 2011. Print.

Hammond, John. *John Hammond on Record.* New York: Summit Books, 1977. Print.

Harmetz, Aljean. *The Making of the Wizard of Oz.* Chicago: Chicago Review Press, Inc., 1977. Print.

Harry, Bill. *The Ringo Starr Encyclopedia.* London: Virgin Books, 2004. Print.

Hauser, Thomas. *Muhammad Ali: His Life and Times.* New York: Simon & Schuster, 1991. Print.

Heatley, Michael. *The Illustrated History of the Electric Guitar.* West Molesey: Merchant Company, Ltd., 2003. Print.

Heffernan, James. "Wolfe's Reading of James Joyce's Ulysses, 1922–1941." *The Modernism Lab at Yale University.* Yale University, 2010. Web. 17 Oct 2014.

Henshaw, Peter. *Mustang.* New York: Chartwell Books, 2013. Print.

Henshaw, Peter. *The Ultimate Encyclopedia of the Corvette.* New York: Chartwell Books, 2004. Print.

"Her Life." *Celebrating Mary Kay Ash 1918–2001.* n.p., n.d. Web. 15 Oct 2014.

"Herschel Walker." *Academy of Achievement.* American Academy of Achievement, 1996–2015. Web. 2 Feb 2015.

Hewett, Caspar. "The Life of Voltaire." *The Great Debate.* C J M Hewett, Aug 2006. Web. 28 Sep 2014.

Heylin, Clinton, ed. *All Yesterday's Parties: The Velvet Underground in Print, 1966–1971.* New York: Da Capo Press, 2005. Print.

Hickok, Ralph. "Koufax, Sandy [Sanford Braun]." *Sports Biographies.* HickockSports.com, 20 Dec 2008. Web. 22 Feb 2015.

Hillenbrand, Laura. *Seabiscuit: An American Legend.* New York: Ballantine Books, 2001. Print.

Hiskey, David. "This Day in History: Robert H. Goddard Performs the First Flight Test of a Liquid Fueled Rocket." *Today I Found Out.* Vacca Foeda Media, 2012. Web. 13 Oct 2014.

Hlavaty, Craig. "8 Years Ago Today: Lakewood Church Moves into Compaq Center." *Houston Chronicle,* 16 Jul 2013. Hearst Newspapers. Web. 19 Jul 2014.

Holden, Stephen. "Johnny Cash, Country Music Bedrock, Dies at 71." *The New York Times.* The New York Times Company, 13 Sep 2003. Web. 29 Sep 2014.

"How It Started." *ESPNFounder.com.* ESPNFounder.com, 2014. Web. 15 Dec 2014.

Howe, Charles. "Where Were You When Greg LeMond Came Back to Win the Tour?" *Velodynamics.* Velodynamics, July 1999. Web. 14 Dec 2014.

"Imagining the Internet: A History and Forecast." *Elon University.* Elon University School of Communications, n.d. Web. 25 Oct 2014.

"Inflation Calculator" *Dollar Times.* HBrothers, 2007–2015. Web. 13 Sep 2015.

"Inventing the Telephone." *ATT.* AT&T Intellectual Property, 2014. Web. 28 Sep 2014.

"Irving Thalberg: Biography." *IMDb.* IMDb.com, Inc., 1990–2014. Web. 14 Oct 2014.

Isaacson, Walter. *Einstein: His Life and Universe.* New York: Simon & Schuster, 2007. Print.

Isaacson, Walter. *Steve Jobs.* New York: Simon & Schuster Paperbacks, 2011. Print.

James, Bill. *Bill James Historical Baseball Abstract.* New York: Villard Books, 1988. Print.

James, Caryn. "Audrey Hepburn, Actress, Is Dead at 63." *The New York Times.* The New York Times Company, 21 Jan 1993. Web. 20 Feb 2015.

"Jim, Do You Know Who Robert Johnson Is?" *Robert Johnson Blues Foundation.* Sony Music Entertainment, 2015. Web. 21 Dec 2008.

"John Coltrane and Eric Dolphy Answer the Jazz Critics." *Downbeat.* Maher Publications, 12 Apr 1962. Web. 30 Nov 2014.

"John Hammond Biography." *Rock and Roll Hall of Fame.* The Rock and Roll Hall of Fame and Museum, Inc., 2014. Web. 29 Sep 2014.

Jones, Carys Wyn. *The Rock Canon: Canonical Values in the Reception of Rock Albums.* Burlington: Ashgate Publishing Company, 2008. Print.

Jones, Jack. "Master of Style, Elegance Was 88: Fred Astaire, Movies' Greatest Dancer, Dies." *Los Angeles Times.* Los Angeles Times, 23 Jun 1987. Web. 23 Oct 2014.

Jordan, David. *Pete Rose: A Biography.* Westport, CT: Greenwood Press, 2004. Print.

Kahn, Ashley. *Kind of Blue: The Making of the Miles Davis Masterpiece.* New York: Da Capo Press, 2001. Print.

Kaminski, Michael. *The Secret History of Star Wars.* Kingston, ON: Legacy Books Press, 2008. Print.

Kashner, Sam. "Here's to You, Mr. Nichols: The Making of *The Graduate.*" *Vanity Fair.* Condé Nast, Mar 2008. Web. 20 July 2014.

Kauffman, Stanford B. *Pan Am Pioneer: A Manager's Memoir from Seaplane Clippers to Jumbo Jets.* Lubbock: Texas Tech University Press, 1995. Print.

Keller, James M. "Beethoven: Symphony No. 9 in D Minor, Opus 125." *San Francisco Symphony.* San Francisco Symphony, Jun 2012. Web. 17 Nov 2014.

Kelley, Kitty. *Oprah.* New York: Crown Publishers, 2010. Print.

Kennedy, Paul, ed. *Favre: The Total Package.* Iola, KS: K. P. Krause Productions, 2008. Print.

"King David." *Jewish Virtual Library.* American-Israeli Cooperative Enterprise, 2014. Web. 17 Oct 2014.

King, Gilbert. "Edison vs. Westinghouse: A Shocking Rivalry." *Smithsonian.com.* The Smithsonian Institution, 11 Oct 2011. Web. 30 Sep 2014.

"Kinko's." *Paul Orfalea.* Paul Orfalea, 2015. Web. 11 Mar 2015.

Knighton, C.S. "Pepys, Samuel (1633–1703), Naval Official and Diarist." *Oxford Dictionary of National Biography.* Oxford University Press, 2004; online edn, Jan 2008. Web. 9 Nov 2014.

Koszarski, Richard. *Hollywood on the Hudson: Film and Television in New York from Griffith to Sarnoff.* Piscataway: Rutgers University Press, 2008. Print.

Lapsley, Phil. "The Greatest 'Bad Business Decision' Quotation That Never Was." *The History of Phone Phreaking Blog.* Phil Lapsley, 8 Jan 2011. Web. 3 Nov 2014.

Layden, Joe. *The Last Great Fight.* New York: St. Martin's Press, 2007. Print.

Leavy, Jane. *Sandy Koufax: A Lefty's Legacy.* New York: HarperCollins Publishers, 2002. Print.

Lebo, Harlan. *Citizen Kane.* New York: Doubleday, 1990. Print.

LeClaire, Jennifer. "Microsoft Laying Internet Explorer to Rest for Good." *CIO Today.* CIO Today Network, 17 Mar 2015. Web. 22 Mar 2015.

"Led Zeppelin Biography." *Rock and Roll Hall of Fame.* The Rock and Roll Hall of Fame and Museum, Inc., 2014. Web. 17 Nov 2014.

"Lee De Forest." *Famous Scientists.* Famous Scientists, 2014. Web. 5 Oct 2014.

"Lee De Forest: Biography." *Bio.* A&E Television Networks, 2014. Web. 5 Oct 2014.

Lee, Stan. *Origins of Marvel Comics.* New York: Marvel Entertainment Group, 1997. Print.

Leiner, Barry M., et al. "Brief History of the Internet." *Internet Society.* Internet Society, 2012. Web. 15 Oct 2012.

Leip, David. "1948 Presidential Election Results." *Dave Leip's Atlas of U.S. Presidential Elections.* David Liep, 2012. Web. 19 Jan 2015.

Lewis, David Levering. *King: A Biography.* Urbana: University of Illinois, 1970. Print.

Lewis, Roger. *The Life and Death of Peter Sellers.* New York: Applause Books, 1997. Print.

Lockwood, Lewis. *Beethoven: The Music & the Life.* New York: W.W. Norton & Company, Inc., 2003. Print.

Lombardi, Mike. "Monomail Defined Future of Flight 75 Years Ago." *Boeing Frontiers Online:* 4.1. Boeing, May 2005. Web. 14 Dec 2015.

"Louis Pasteur and Rabies Vaccination." *Institut Pasteur.* Institut Pasteur, 27 May 2013. Web. 29 Sep 2014.

Low, Chris. "Harper Emerges from Backup Role to Become History-making QB." *ESPN.* ESPN Internet Ventures, 12 Nov 2007. Web. 5 Oct 2014.

Manso, Peter. *Brando: The Biography.* New York: Hyperion, 1994. Print.

"Margaret Thatcher." *New World Encyclopedia.* New World Encyclopedia, 5 Oct 2014. Web. 1 Feb 2015.

"Margaret Thatcher: A Life in Words." *The Telegraph.* Telegraph Media Group Limited, 4 Apr 2013. Web. 1 Feb 2015.

"Marker #5-62: First Ship-to-Shore Broadcast." *Remarkable Ohio.* n.p,. n.d. Web. 3 Oct 2014.

Martin, George. *All You Need Is Ears: The Inside Personal Story of the Genius Who Created the Beatles.* New York: St. Martin's Press, 1979. Print.

Mathison, Keith. "Luther, Calvin, and Copernicus — A Reformed Approach to Science and Scripture." *Ligonier.org.* Ligonier Ministries, 1 Jun 2012. Web. 17 Oct 2014.

McCullough, David. *1776.* New York: Simon & Schuster, 2005. Print.

McCullough, David. *Truman.* New York: Simon & Schuster, 1992. Print.

McDonough, John. "John Hammond: The Ear of an Oracle." *NPR.org.* NPR, 15 Dec 2010. Web. 29 Sep 2014.

Meacham, Jon. *Franklin and Winston: An Intimate Portrait of an Epic Friendship.* New York: Random House, 2003. Print.

Mendelsohn, John. "Led Zeppelin I." *Rolling Stone.* Rolling Stone, 15 March 1969. Web. 15 Oct 2014.

Mezger, Raelyn. "Seabiscuit: An American Legend." *Thoroughbred Greats.* Thoroughbred Greats, 2012. Web. 16 Nov 2014.

"Mike Tyson." *Bio.* A&E Television Networks, 2015. Web. 19 Feb 2015.

Moffat, Charles. "Vincent Van Gogh." *The Art History Archive — Biography & Paintings.* n.p., May 2007. Web. 29 Sep 2014.

Morton, David. "Exploring the History of the Recording Business." *Recording History.* David Morton, 1998–2006. Web. 20 Feb 2015

"Movie Franchises." *The Numbers.* Nash Information Services, LLC., 1997–2015. Web. 15 Dec 2015.

Nack, William. S*ecretariat: The Making of a Champion.* New York: Da Capo Press Books, 2002. Print.

Nemy, Enid. "Mary Kay Ash, Who Built a Cosmetics Empire and Adored Pink, Is Dead at 83." *The New York Times.* The New York Times Company, 23 Nov 2001. Web. 15 Oct 2014.

"New Global Survey Ranks CNN as Top International News Brand." *CNN Press Room.* Cable News Network, 16 Oct 2014. Web. 26 Oct 2014.

"New York Yankees." *Baseball Almanac.* Baseball Almanac, Inc., 2000–2014. Web. 6 Oct 2014.

Newcomb, Simon. "Is the Airship Coming?" *McClure's Magazine,* 17 Sep 1901. Mississippi State University Library, 2015. Web. 21 Feb 2015.

Nilsson, Jeff. "75 Years Ago: Snow White's Premiere." *Saturday Evening Post.* Saturday Evening Post Society, 15 Dec 2012. Web. 30 Sep 2014.

Norman, Phillip. *Shout!: The Beatles in Their Generation.* New York: Simon & Schuster, 1981. Print.

Oates, Stephen B. *William Faulkner: The Man and the Artist.* New York: Harper & Row, 1987. Print.

O'Connell, T.S. "Yankee Stadium: One of the Crown Jewels Has Seen Its Fair Share of History." *Yankee Legacy.* Steiner Sports, Inc., n.d. Web. 6 Oct 2014.

"Oct 20, 1968: Fosbury Flops to an Olympic Record." *History.* A&E Television Networks, LLC., 2014. Web. 23 Nov 2014.

Orfalea, Paul and Ann Marsh. *Copy This: Lessons from a Hyperactive Dyslexic Who Turned a Bright Idea into a Company Called Kinko's.* New York: Workman Publishing, Inc., 2007. Print.

Osteen, Joel. *Become a Better You.* New York: Howard Books, 2008. Print.

O'Toole, Garson. "Beatles Rejection: We Don't Like Their Sound. Groups of Guitars Are on Their Way Out." *Quote Investigator.* Garson O'Toole, 27 Apr 2013. Web. 17 Oct 2014.

O'Toole, Garson. "Can't Act; Slightly Bald; Can Dance a Little." *Quote Investigator.* Garson O'Toole, 7 Aug 2014. Web. 17 Oct 2014.

O'Toole, Garson. "I Will Send a Barrel of This Wonderful Whiskey to Every General in the Army." *Quote Investigator.* Garson O'Toole, 28 Feb 2013. Web. 26 Jan 2014.

"Over the Rainbow's Enduring Appeal." *BBCNews.com.* BBC, 15 Mar 2006. Web. 11 Jan 2015.

Panabaker, James. *Shelby Foote and the Art of History: Two Gates to the City.* Knoxville: University of Tennessee Press, 2004. Print.

"Pauline Kael Reviews A–Z." *Geocities.com.* n.p., n.d. Web. 2 Feb 2015.

Peck, Janice. *The Age of Oprah: Cultural Icon for the Neoliberal Era.* Boulder: Paradigm Publishers, 2008. Print.

PennLive Editorial Board. "Retraction for Our 1863 Editorial Calling Gettysburg Address 'Silly Remarks': Editorial." *Penn Live: The Patriot-News.* PA Media Group, 24 Nov 2013. Web. 20 Jan 2014.

Pentland, William. "The Man Who Bought the Persian Gulf." *Forbes.* Forbes.com, LLC, 23 Feb 2011. Web. 11 Nov 2014.

Pepys, Samuel. "Monday 29 September 1662." *The Diary of Samuel Pepys M.A. F.R.S.* Covent Garden: George Bell & Sons, 1893. N. pag. *The Diary of Samuel Pepys: Daily Entries from the 17th Century Diary.* Pepysdiary.com, Jan 2003. Web. 21 Feb 2015.

"Pete Rose's Records." *Lifttheban.net.* Lift The Ban, 2013. Web. 19 Oct 2014.

"Peyton Manning Likely Will Never Play Football Again, Sources Say." *Los Angeles Times.* Los Angeles Times, 31 Jan 2012. Web. 11 Jul 2014.

"Peyton Manning." *Official Site of the Denver Broncos.* Denver Broncos, 2014. Web. 22 Oct 2014.

Phaidon Editors and Bruce Altchuler. *Exhibitions That Made Art History, Volume 1.* New York: Phaidon Press, Inc., 2008. Print.

Pringle, Patrick. *The Young Einstein.* New York: Roy Publishers, 1965. Print.

Ratliff, Ben. *Coltrane: The Story of a Sound.* New York: Farrar, Straus, and Giroux, 2007. Print.

Rebello, Kathy with Amy Cortese and Rob Hof. "Inside Microsoft." *Business Week.* Bloomberg L.P., 15 Jul 1996. Web. 2 Nov 2014.

Revis, Layla. "How to Think Like a Revolutionary." *The Huffington Post.* TheHuffingtonPost.com, Inc., 22 Apr 2012. Web. 23 Nov 2014.

Rewald, John. *Georges Seurat.* New York: Wittenberk & Company, 1946. Print.

Ridley, Mark. *The Cooperative Gene: How Mendel's Demon Explains the Evolution of Complex Beings.* New York: The Free Press, 2001. Print.

"Robert E. Lee." *HistoryNet.* Weider History, 2014. Web. 17 Nov 2014.

Robinson, David. *Chaplin, The Mirror of Opinion.* Bloomington: Indiana University Press, 1983. Print.

Robinson, David. *Chaplin: His Life and Art.* London: Paladin Books, 1985. Print.

Robinson, Scott R. "The English Theatre, 1642–1800." *Central Washington University.* Scott R. Robinson, 2000–2010. Web. 19 Jan 2015.

"Rolling Stones' Tour Breaks Attendance Records." *Huliq.* n.p., 10 Oct 2007. Web. 28 Sep 2014.

Roper, Elmo. "It's Dewey Over Truman by a Landslide." *The Evening Independent [St. Augustine]* 9 Sep 1948, 41st ed., sec. 266: 1–2. *Google News*. Google. Web. 7 Oct 2014.

Rothschild, Richard. "A Look Back at Cassius Clay's Upset of Sonny Liston 50 Years Ago." *Sports Illustrated.* Time Inc., 25 Feb 2014, updated 10 Jun 2014. Web. 17 Nov 2014.

Rubin, Gretchen. *Forty Ways to Look at Winston Churchill.* New York: Random House, 2004. Print.

Rucker, James "Sparky." "Robert Johnson and the Roots of the Delta Blues." *Sparkyandrhonda.com.* James "Sparky" Rucker, Jun 1999. Web. 30 Sep 2014.

"Rudyard Kipling." *Poetry Foundation.* Poetry Foundation, 2014. Web. 16 Nov 2014.

Russell, Douglas S. "Orders, Decorations and Medals." *The Orders, Decorations and Medals of Sir Winston Churchill.* London: Brassey's, Ltd., 1996. Excerpt in *The Churchill Centre.* Churchill Centre, 2014. Web. 29 Sep 2014.

Sacks, Ethan. "Spider-Man Got His Start as a Fly on the Wall of Marvel's Stan Lee." *NYDailyNews.com.* NYDailyNews.com, 27 Jun 2012. Web. 30 Sep 2014.

Sandburg, Carl. *Abraham Lincoln: The Prairie Years and the War Years.* New York: Sterling Publishing, 2007. Print.

"Sandy Koufax." *Baseball-reference.com.* Sports Reference LLC, 2000–2014. Web. 30 Sep 2014.

Scaduto, Anthony. "Bob Dylan: An Intimate Biography, Part One." *Rolling Stone.* Rolling Stone, 2 Mar 1972. Web. 30 Nov 2014.

Scarfone, Jay and William Skillman. *The Wizard of Oz: The Official 75th Anniversary Companion.* New York: Harper's Design, 2013. Print.

Schaap, Jeremy. "Busting the Myths of Tyson-Douglas." *ESPN.com.* ESPN Internet Ventures, 12 Feb 2010. Web. 29 Sep 2014.

Schoenherr, Steve. "Recording Technology History." *Audio Engineering Society.* Steven E. Schoenherr, 1995–2005. Web. 3 Oct 2014.

Schwartz, Larry. "Total Domination." *ESPN.com.* ESPN Internet Ventures, n.d. Web. 31 Jan 2015.

"Seurat and the Making of La Grande Jatte." *The Art Institute of Chicago.* The Art Institute of Chicago, 2003. Web. 18 Nov 2014.

Severo, Richard. "For Fitzgerald's Works, It's Roaring 70's." *The New York Times.* The New York Times Company, 3 Mar 1974. Web. 30 Sep 2014.

Shapiro, Susan. "Regrets, Even Critics Have a Few." *The Wall Street Journal.* Dow Jones & Company, Inc., 11 Sep 2012. Web. 17 Oct 2012.

Shawbel, Dan. "Paul Orfalea on Creating the Kinko's Brand." Interview. *Forbes.* Forbes.com, LLC, 28 Jun 2012. Web. 11 Mar 2015.

Shelokhonov, Steve. "Led Zeppelin Biography." *IMDb.* IMDb.com, Inc., 1990–2014. Web. 17 Nov 2014.

Shontell, Allison. "The Amazing Story of How Steve Jobs Took Apple from Near Bankruptcy to Billions in 13 Years." *Business Insider.* Business Insider Inc., 19 Jan 2011. Web. 20 Jan 2014.

Singham, Mano. "The Copernican Myths." *Physics Today,* Dec 2007: 48–49. *Sheboygan Area School District*. SASD. Web. 7 Jul 2014.

Sinitiere, Phillip Luke. "From the Oasis of Love to Your Best Life Now: A Brief History of Lakewood Church." *Houston History,* Summer 2011: 2–9. *Houston History*. Houston History Magazine, Oct 2011. Web. 7 Jul 2014.

Smith, Loran with Lewis Grizzard. *Glory, Glory.* Atlanta: Peachtree Publishing, 1981. Print.

"Snow White and the Seven Dwarves." *Movie-Film-Review.* Chris Tookey, 2009–2014. Web. 8 Jul 2014.

"Sonny Liston." *BoxRec.* Boxrec, n.d. Web. 17 Nov 2014.

"Sophia Loren: Biography." *Bio.* A&E Television Networks, 2014. Web. 30 Sep 2014.

Sousanis, John. "World Vehicle Population Tops 1 Billion Units." *WardsAuto.com.* Penton, 15 Aug 2011. Web. 8 Jul 2014.

Spalding, Francis. *Roger Fry: Art and Life.* Oakland, CA: University of California Press, 1980. Print.

"Spider-Man in Other Media." *Wikipedia.* Wikimedia, 2015. Web. 27 Jan 2015.

Spitz, Bob. *Dylan: A Biography.* New York: W.W. Norton, 1989. Print.

Sterman, Paul. "Meet 'Kinko' Paul Orfalea." *Ability.* Ability Magazine, 1995–2015. Web. 11 Mar 2015.

"Stick to Truck Driving." *Snopes.com.* Snopes.com, 26 Apr 2007. Web. 4 Nov 2014.

Stump, Al. *Cobb.* Chapel Hill, NC: Algonquin Books, 1994. Print.

Swift, E. M. "Le Grand LeMond Greg LeMond, 1989 Sportsman of the Year, Rewrote His Own Legend with a Heroic Comeback and a Magnificent Finish in the Tour de France." *Sports Illustrated* 25 Dec 1989: n. pag. *SI.com.* Time Inc., 2014. Web. 7 Dec 2014.

"Ted Turner & CNN." *The Pop History Dig.* The Pop History Dig, LLC, 29 Nov 2008. Last updated 30 Aug 2014. Web. 22 Oct 2014.

"Telephone History: The Early Years — 1876–1900." *Telephony Museum.* Gregory R. Russell, 1998–2012. Web. 1 Feb 2015.

"Television Viewing (Most Recent) by Country." *NationMaster.* NationMaster.com, 2003–2015. Web. 27 Jan 2015.

"Televisions (Most Recent) by Country." *NationMaster.* NationMaster.com, 2003–2015. Web. 27 Jan 2015.

"Tesla: Life and Legacy — Harnessing Niagara." *PBS.* Public Broadcasting Service, 1995–2014. Web. 30 Sep 2014.

"The Babbage Engine: Dionysius Lardner." *Computer History Museum.* Computer History Museum, 2008. Web. 3 Oct 2014.

"The Gettysburg Address." *AbrahamLincolnOnline.org.* Abraham Lincoln Online, 2014. Web. 28 Sep 2014.

"The Gettysburg Address." *History.* A&E Television Networks, LLC, 2014. Web. 28 Sep 2014.

"The History of the Edison Cylinder Phonograph." *The Library of Congress.* The Library of Congress, n.d. Web. 29 Sep 2014.

"The Jack Paar Show (1961)." *Barbara Streisand Archives.* Matt Howe, 2014. Web. 17 Nov 2014.

"The Luckiest Football Game Ever Won: The True Story of Super Bowl III." *Super Bowl III.* Superbowl3.net, 2012. Web. 30 Sep 2014.

"The Modality of Miles Davis and John Coltrane." *W. W. Norton & Company, Inc.* W.W. Norton and Company, Inc., 2014. Web. 28 Sep 2014.

"The Montgomery Bus Boycott: They Changed the World." *The Montgomery Bus Boycott.* Www.montgomeryadvertiser.com, 2013. Web. 7 Oct 2014.

"The Nipper Saga." *Designboom.* Designboom, 2000–2010. Web. 5 Oct 2014.

"The Nobel Prize in Literature 1953." *Nobelprize.org.* Nobel Media AB, 2014. Web. 19 Feb 2015.

"The Richest People in America 2014." *Forbes.* Forbes.com, LLC, 2015. Web. 20 Jan 2015.

"The Rolling Stones Still Rocking 50 Years After 1st Gig." *City News Toronto.* Rogers Media, 12 Jul 2012. Web. 15 Oct 2014.

"The Sound of Music Named the Greatest Musical of All Time." *Thaindian News.* Thaindian.com Company, 11 Dec 2007. Web. 19 Feb 2015.

"The Ultimate Chatfest." *Oprah.com.* Harpo Productions, Inc., 25 Feb 2011. Web. 7 July 2014.

"The Unlikely Casting of Dustin Hoffman in *The Graduate.*" *AMC.* AMC Network Entertainment LLC, Apr 2008. Web. 1 Feb 2015.

"The Velvet Underground Biography." *Musician Biographies.* Net Industries, 2015. Web. 2 Feb 2015.

"The War of the Currents: AC vs. DC Power." *Energy.gov.* U.S. Department of Energy, 20 Nov 2013. Web. 30 Sep 2014.

Theoharis, Jeanne. *The Rebellious Life of Mrs. Rosa Parks.* Boston: Beacon Press, 2013. Print.

"Thomas Alva Edison Biography." *The Thomas Edison Papers.* Rutgers, The State University of New Jersey, updated 20 Feb 2012. Web. 6 Oct 2014.

Thomas, Henry. *Thomas Alva Edison.* New York: Van Rees Press, 1958. Print.

"Trail of the Hellhound: Son House." *National Park Service.* Department of the Interior, 2001. Web. 3 Oct 2014.

Trento, Salvatore. "Banks Four Leagues in the Air: The Ives Expedition up the Colorado River." *Gorp.com.* Orbitz Away LLC, 29 Apr 2002. Web. 14 Oct 2014.

"Truckline Café." *IBDB: Internet Broadway Database.* The Broadway League, 2001–2014. Web. 30 Sep 2014.

Turnbull, Martin. "Hollywood Timeline." *Martin Turnbull.* Martin Turnbull, 2014. Web. 6 Nov 2014.

"Ty Cobb." *Baseball Hall of Fame.* National Baseball Hall of Fame and Museum, 2014. Web. 30 Sep 2014.

Ullman, Agnes. "Pasteur-Koch: Distinctive Ways of Thinking about Infectious Diseases." *Microbe Magazine.* American Society for Microbiology, Aug 2007. Web. 30 Sep 2014.

Van Luling, Todd. "8 Things You Didn't Know About James Bond." *Huffington Post.* TheHuffingtonPost.com, Inc., 27 Nov 2014. Web. 19 Jan 2015.

Vincent, Alice. "The Beatles' Please Please Me, 50 Years On — 10 Facts About the Debut Album." *The Telegraph.* Telegraph Media Group Limited. 22 Mar 2013. Web. 9 Sep 2015

"Voltaire, Shakespeare, and Canada." *Canadian Adaptations of Shakespeare Project.* Daniel Fischlin, 2004. Web. 28 Sep 2014.

Wahlberg, Bjorn. "United Artists Rejection Letter." *Starwarz.com.* Starkiller, 4 Mar 2010. Web. 8 Nov 2014.

Wald, Elijah. *Escaping the Delta: Robert Johnson and the Invention of the Blues.* New York: HarperCollins Publishers, 2004. Print.

Walker, Audrey. *Audrey: Her Real Story.* New York: St. Martin's Press, 1994. Print.

"Walker, Herschel." *Contemporary Black Biography.* Encyclopedia,com, 2009. Web. 19 Feb 2015

"Walt Disney." *Bio.* A&E Television Networks, 2015. Web. 19 Feb 2015.

Weber, Jack. "Microsoft Internet Explorer." *MacUser.* Sep 1996. Web. 2 Nov 2014.

Weintraub, Robert. *The House That Ruth Built: A New Stadium, the First Yankees Championship, and the Redemption of 1923.* Boston: Little, Brown and Company, 2011. Print.

White, Dana. *George Lucas.* Minneapolis: Lerner Publications Company, 2000. Print.

Whittemore, Hank. *CNN: The Inside Story.* Boston: Little, Brown and Company, 1980. Print.

Widmer, Ted. "The Other Gettysburg Address." *The New York Times.* The New York Times Company, 19 Nov 2013. Web. 28 Sep 2014.

Wikisource Contributors. "The New York Times/Robert Goddard." *Wikisource.* Wikisource, 22 Jun 2012. Web. 21 Feb 2015.

"William Faulkner: Biography." *Bio.* A&E Television Networks, 2015. Web. 19 Feb 2015.

"Wilma (Glodean) Rudolph (1940–1994)." *Bio.* A&E Television Networks, 2015. Web. 31 Jan 2015.

Woideck, Carl. *Charlie Parker: His Music and Life.* Ann Arbor: University of Michigan Press, 1998. Print.

"Women in History — Wilma Rudolph." *Women in History Ohio.* n.p., 2014. Web. 21 Feb 2015.

"World's Most Expensive Paintings." *Ivan Krutoyarov.com.* Ivan Krutoyarov, 2010–2013. Web. 19 Jan 2015.

Wyatt, Robert and John Andrew Johnson, ed. *The George Gershwin Reader.* New York: Oxford University Press, 2004. Print.

Wyman, Bill. *Rolling with the Stones.* New York: DK Publishing, Inc., 2002. Print.

"Xerox 2013 Annual Report." *Xerox.* Xerox Corporation, 2014. Web. 26 Oct 2014.

Yarow, Jay. "Here's What Steve Ballmer Thought About the iPhone Five Years Ago." *Business Insider.* Business Insider Inc., 29 Jun 2012. Web. 25 Jan 2015.

Yates, Ronald E. "Douglas KO's Tyson in 10." *Chicago Tribune.* Chicagotribune.com, 11 Feb 1990. Web. 29 Sep 2014.

Yergin, Daniel. *The Prize: The Epic Quest for Oil, Money & Power.* New York: Simon & Schuster, 1991. Google E-book.

"Yogi Berra." *St. Louis Sports Hall of Fame.* Above Web Media, 2013. Web. 30 Sep 2014.

York, Kyle. "Herschel Walker (b. 1962)." *New Georgia Encyclopedia.* Georgia Humanities Council and the University of Georgia Press, 11 Nov 2005. Web. 19 Nov 2014.

"You Ain't Seen Nothin' Yet." *Variety.* Variety Media, LLC, 16 Oct 2005. Web. 4 Nov 2014.

Zall, Paul M. "Scouring the Text of Lamon's Recollections." *Journal of the Abraham Lincoln Association,* Volume 30, Issue 2, Summer 2009, pp. 81–85. Board of Trustees of the University of Illinois. Web. 17 Nov 2014.

Zemel, Carol M. *The Formation of a Legend: Van Gogh Criticism 1890–1920.* Ann Arbor: UMI Press, 1980. Print.

Zimaneck, Brad. "Revenge Is Sweet: Favre Dismantles Team That Traded Him." *JSOnline.com.* Journal Sentinel Inc., 1995. Web. 2 Dec 2014.

About the Author

G.R. HOWARD is Georgian by birth, and currently living in Dallas by way of Los Angeles and Portland. When not writing and earning a living, he spends most of his time with two old convertibles and his much-beloved 1964 Vox amplifier.

www.ingramcontent.com/pod-product-compliance
Lightning Source LLC
Chambersburg PA
CBHW060154070426
42447CB00033B/1338